## PAUL D

Paul Davies is a physicist and writer who has lived in South Australia since 1990. He has held academic appointments in Cambridge, London, Newcastle upon Tyne, and Adelaide, and is currently Visiting Professor at Imperial College London. He has gained an international reputation as a lucid expositor of science and philosophy, having written a string of best-selling books, and contributed to hundreds of television and radio programs around the world. Among his best-known works are the Eureka Prize-winning *The Mind of God*, *About Time* and *Are We Alone?* His forthcoming book *The Fifth Miracle* offers a penetrating new look at the origin of life. In 1995, Davies won the Templeton Prize for Progress in Religion — the world's largest prize — for his lifelong exploration of the deeper significance of science.

## PHILLIP ADAMS

The infinitely curious Phillip Adams AO comperes ABC Radio National's 'Late Night Live' and writes two columns for the *Australian*. As well, he is an author, a film- and documentary-maker, and has chaired a wide range of organisations and committees. He has written countless millions of words for everything from Melbourne's *Communist Guardian* to London's *Sunday Times*. Among his books are the *Unspeakable Adams*, *Adams Versus God*, the hugely successful series of joke books with Patrice Newell, *The Retreat from Tolerance* (as editor), and *Talkback* (with Lee Burton). Films he produced in the 1970s and 1980s include many that are now considered classics of Australian cinema, including *The Adventures of Barry McKenzie*, *Don's Party*, *We of the Never-Never*, and *The Getting of Wisdom*.

# *Paul* DAVIES

in conversation with *Phillip* ADAMS

# MORE
# *Big*
# *Questions*

ABC
BOOKS

Published by ABC Books for the
AUSTRALIAN BROADCASTING CORPORATION
GPO Box 9994 Sydney NSW 2001

Copyright © Piper Films 1998

Copyright © Front cover photograph Piper Films 1998

*First published May 1988*

All rights reserved. No part of this publication
may be reproduced, stored in a retrieval system
or transmitted in any form or by any means,
electronic, mechanical, photocopying, recording
or otherwise, without the prior written permission
of the Australian Broadcasting Corporation.

National Library of Australia
Cataloguing-in-Publication entry

Davies, P. C. W. (Paul Charles William), 1946– .

More big questions: Paul Davies in conversation
with Phillip Adams

ISBN 0 7333 0668 3.

1. Davies, P. C. W. (Paul Charles William), 1946–  Interviews.
2. Metaphysics. 3. Time. 4. Life on other planets.
5. Cosmology. 6. End of the universe. 7. Space and time.
8. Consciousness. 9. Religion and science.
I. Adams, Phillip, 1939– .
II. Australian Broadcasting Corporation. III. Title.

110

*Designed by Brash Design Pty Ltd*
*Illustrated by Eckermann Art and Design*
*Cover design by RENO Design Group*

*Set in 10/18pt Slimbach by Brash Design Pty Ltd*
*Printed and bound in Australia by*
*Australian Print Group, Maryborough, Victoria*

2 4 5 3 1

# FOREWORD

IT SEEMED TO ME A SUPERLATIVE THING —
TO KNOW THE EXPLANATION
OF EVERYTHING, WHY IT COMES TO BE,
WHY IT PERISHES, WHY IT IS.

❖

SO SPOKE SOCRATES nearly 2500 years ago, and we're still at it. Paul Davies and Phillip Adams, I picture them in simple togas, sitting in chairs and musing on the meaning of life.

And what a good time to do it: after a century of stupendous intellectual achievement in science we are now asking 'how much is left to know' and 'are we near the end — the end of physics, perhaps the end of most big questions'.

Hence the recurrence of TOEs (Theories of Everything) and GUTs (Grand Unified Theories). Hence also the rise of credulity, fringe science and the irrational as some folk opt for simpler explanations or shove back against the scientific juggernaut. Douglas Hofstadter said 'Irrationality is

# FOREWORD

the square root of all evil.' Alan Turing remarked, almost in reply that 'Science is a differential equation. Religion a boundary condition'.

I came across both statements in John Barrow's *Theories of Everything* — which leads one to ask: why should we want to read a conversation between two Oz-based intellectual omnivores ranging far and wide when, instead, we could pick up any number of authors, such as Barrow, who have distilled many of these Big Questions into dense marching prose?

Two reasons. First, this book gives such a broad, accessible introduction — a Martian's eye-view of what it's all about. From this we can then go to the specialised works, thirsting for more. Second, Paul and Phillip are unique fellows, and I can say this having known both for decades: for them the concepts are pre-eminent. This is not two cleversticks banging away from on high but two deeply curious and well-informed polymaths very much in love with ideas and how to share them. The enthusiasm resonates, even on the page.

Paul Davies is a well-educated Englishman who was swept along by the incredible excitement of space exploration and molecular biology in the 1950s and early 1960s. For him, a career in science became inevitable and he went on to Cambridge and the University of Newcastle in the UK. Phillip Adams, by contrast, had no university training, and

FOREWORD

I use that word on purpose because a *trained* mind usually won't dare do what Phillip does, leaping across boundaries, confessing wide-eyed, unblushing naivety, urging for further explanation because he really wants to know.

Know where life came from, where consciousness begins, why the very small is very odd, and what happens next, after Einstein, after the material world.

Phillip Adams, like me, is an atheist: he has no evidence that God exists; Paul Davies is not so sure but sees a universe organised in such a rare and particular way that he is inclined to imagine, at least for a while, that there must be more to it. His contributions to this field won him the Templeton Prize for contributions to religious thought, an award worth even more than the Nobel!

So you are in good company. Conversation on a cosmic scale. Which reminds me of one last maxim beloved of John Barrow, a piece of graffiti found in Texas and signed by the ever-industrious 'Anonymous': 'Time is God's way of keeping things from happening all at once.'

*Robyn Williams*
Sydney, February 1998

# CONTENTS

❖

1 SCIENCE AND TRUTH *11*

2 IN SEARCH OF EDEN *33*

3 ARE WE ALONE IN THE UNIVERSE? *60*

4 DOES GOD PLAY DICE? *85*

5 EINSTEIN'S LEGACY *112*

6 COSMIC BUTTERFLIES *136*

❖

ONE

# SCIENCE AND TRUTH

FOR MILLENNIA, *human beings have wondered at their own existence, gazing up at the night skies with a mixture of awe and dread. They have sought to find a meaning to their lives, a power to commute their death sentence, an author for all existence. And the answers to their questions came from priests and prophets, from mythologies and theologies. More recently, powerful answers — and entirely new questions — have been provided by mathematics and science, by cosmology, biology and physics.*

*Since Galileo's little difficulties with the church, there has been a great battle between fact and faith. Now, as we exit a century and a millennium, a new generation of physicists are predicting unprecedented revelations, promising a 'Theory of Everything', and a glimpse of 'the face of God'.*

*As the lines between the physicist and the theologian blur, as each seems intent on appropriating the territory, and the language, of the other, we talk to Paul Davies about the mysteries that have filled people with fascination and dread since the dawn of human time — and we pose new questions deriving from the powerful equations of*

MORE BIG QUESTIONS

*mathematics and by the realms discovered through micro-scope and telescope.*

*It required faith to accept the answers to the big questions provided by religion. Is it much different with science? Can the lay person begin to understand what science is telling us, when it is so improbable, so beyond belief? For most of us the idea of time and space beginning with a big bang, and the hypothesis of parallel universes, are incomprehensible.*

*In this book, we put the big questions, old and new, to a scientist, to see whether we can make sense of what science is telling us. Or are we to take science on faith?*

*Welcome to a world where only Monty Python and Alice in Wonderland could feel at home. Welcome to the counter-intuitive world of Paul Davies.*

**Phillip:**

Paul Davies, we have six chances in which to discuss such minor matters as the origins of life, whether God plays dice with the universe, and whether we're alone in that universe. But before we tackle them I want you to defend science from its critics — and there are a great many of them. We look back on a century of scientific triumph, triumphalism, and hubris. The atom has been split, we've bounced on the moon, our technologies are nibbling at the edge of space, and we've discovered the double helix of DNA. And yet

## SCIENCE AND TRUTH

voices are raised against science, from left and right, from feminists and theologians, from the New Age. Let's look at some of the criticisms and see whether they're justified. One of the most common is that science is guilty of the sin of reductionism. What is that sin?

Paul:

If you're faced with a complicated problem, it is very tempting to chop it up into a lot of simple problems, and then knock them off one by one. It is sometimes claimed that if you have solved all the simple problems you've solved the whole thing. That's reductionism in a nutshell. And as a methodology it works extremely well. In my discipline, which is physics, it's had some amazing successes. Look at the world about us, just see how complicated it is, the richness and diversity of nature. How are we ever to come to understand it? Well, a good way to start is by breaking it up into small bite-sized pieces.

One example is atomism. The belief that the entire universe is made up of atoms, or some sort of fundamental particles, and that everything that happens in nature is just the rearrangement of these particles, has proved extraordinarily fruitful. Once you focus down to the level of individual atoms you can work out all the laws and principles that govern them. You can figure out in detail what they are doing. It's then tempting to believe that if you understand

MORE BIG QUESTIONS

individual atoms and the way they interact, you understand everything. But of course it's a fallacy! It's often called the fallacy of 'nothing buttery' — to say that the world is 'nothing but' a collection of atoms or subatomic particles interacting with each other. However, this just isn't true. So many of the qualities of the world around us simply can't be understood at the atomic level. I don't mean just a dramatic thing like life, but even something as basic and prosaic as the wetness of water. You have to take into account the collective and organisational aspects of matter to get the whole picture. But there is this great temptation, because reductionism works so well, because you get quick and easy answers using it as a methodology, to suppose that it tells the whole story.

Physics has cured itself of this reductionist slant in the twentieth century. It's now gone beyond reductionism, which worked so well in the nineteenth century. There are aspects of physics now, things to do with lasers and superconductors and phenomena involving large numbers of particles and so on, where you simply can't get by with looking only at the individual entities out of which things are built. By contrast, biology is going through a very reductionist phase at the moment. Consider something as complicated as the living organism. How can you understand it? Well, you might start by looking at its cells. How can you understand its cells? They are still immensely complex. You go the next step and

SCIENCE AND TRUTH

look at the molecules within the cells. By following this procedure, you get quick answers, enormously impressive answers, and it's very beguiling to suppose that life is about nothing but molecules interacting with each other. Yet I think this is an incomplete picture of reality.

**Phillip:**

The lay critic of science often uses reductionism differently, condemning science in its totality for taking, if you like, the ghost out of the machine.

**Paul:**

What you are really referring to is demystification. I think there is a difference between reductionism and demystification. It's the job of the scientist to explain the world, which is mysterious when you start out. If you explain some aspect of it then you have demystified it. Some people think that nature is somehow diminished when it is explained. They prefer the romance of the mystery, and would like some things about nature to be left alone. A lot of people say, for example, 'we don't want to know how life began' or 'we don't want to know about the causes of consciousness' or 'we don't want to know how the universe came into existence' because if these things are explained, they are considered to be explained *away*. Again, there is confusion between explaining something and explaining it away, a

MORE BIG QUESTIONS

belief that if we can write down a set of equations or a set of principles that tells us how a phenomenon happened then we've lost something; some quality has gone out of it.

Let me give you an example. Life is something that is important to us. I'm living, you're living — we're surrounded by living things. We feel that the quality of being alive is such an important thing. But suppose biologists tell us that living organisms are *nothing but* collections of molecules interacting in complicated ways, that there is nothing more to it than that. Have we, so to speak, sapped away the essence of life? Have we exorcised the ghost from the machine? And if so, does that in some way diminish us, and the living organisms in the world about us? Well, I personally don't think so. I believe that is a mistaken way to look at what science aims to achieve. In my opinion, science actually *increases* the wonder because it not only explains the world, it shows us how truly remarkable nature really is. Surely, it is much better for us to behold the wonder and ingenuity of nature exposed by the spotlight of knowledge than for us to hide in the corners of ignorance?

**Phillip:**

I agree with you. I have always found that science increases one's sense of awe of the numinous. But let's look at another criticism, this time the feminist's criticism, that science is essentially patriarchal.

SCIENCE AND TRUTH

**Paul:**

I have a lot of sympathy with women who complain that science is dominated by men. It is. Frankly, most famous scientists are Dead White Males. One need only think of Newton, Galileo, Darwin and so on. However, you mustn't confuse scientists with science. Science itself belongs to everybody. It just happens, for reasons of historical accident, that European men invented science and have dominated it for the last 300 years. Actually, that is increasingly changing, though I admit it is still very difficult to get women to come into science. The problem seems not so much to be that women scientists are discriminated against, but that young girls just don't seem to be interested in science in the way that scientists would like them to be. There are undeniably problems here — educational, sociological and professional — that feminists have correctly identified. But these are not problems with science itself.

You could, after all, make the same criticism of mathematics. Most famous mathematicians are also Dead White Males. Pythagoras was a Greek man, but that doesn't mean that there is anything suspect about Pythagoras's theorem. Pythagoras's theorem is true whoever discovers it. It's there for everybody to use — it's pancultural. I don't think that anybody would seriously argue that mathematics is somehow culturally relative or the product of a male conspiracy. Pythagoras's theorem is simply a true state-

MORE BIG QUESTIONS

ment of geometry, and any woman can prove it to her satisfaction.

**Phillip:**

There is, of course, a more general criticism that science is culturally biased. Many ethnic groups would argue that science is very much dominated by Western European traditions.

**Paul:**

They are quite right, but there are good historical reasons for this. Science as we know it today came out of Western Europe and many of its procedures — indeed, the entire world view of science — undeniably draws upon the European tradition. If you look back at how science originated, it rests upon twin pillars. The first is Greek philosophy, with its emphasis on the ability of human beings to understand their world through the use of rational reasoning. The second is monotheistic religion — Judaism, Christianity and Islam — with its emphasis on a created world that is ordered by a Designer in a rational and intelligible way. Those were the dominant influences that gave rise to science in seventeenth-century Europe. Science as we now know it didn't happen in any other part of the world, and it is fascinating to wonder why not. If you look, for example, at the situation in China at the time of Newton, their technology was much more advanced. However, the Chinese didn't understand

SCIENCE AND TRUTH

the *principles* on which their technology was based. It was a sort of trial and error development. The same was true of all earlier cultures. By contrast, what happened in seventeenth-century Europe was that the first scientists began to understand how nature works, and so they were able to design their technology according to the principles that they had discovered. It's a matter of historical fact that this way of doing things came out of Europe. Now that doesn't mean science is culturally relative, that because it is a product of European culture it is relevant only to the European mind. Like mathematics, science is there for everybody to use. The Chinese can use the same science as Europeans now, and they do!

**Phillip:**

Later we will be contemplating whether or not life exists in other nooks and crannies of the universe. Let's imagine we come upon a group of scientists practising on Mars, to our general astonishment. Will their science be the same as your science? Would the science hypothetically practised in the farthest flung corner of the Milky Way necessarily be the same science as ours?

**Paul:**

Yes it would! Actually, there are two questions here. One is: might this hypothetical group of alien scientists be interested

MORE BIG QUESTIONS

in the same problems as us? Perhaps not. They might be doing the science of things that just don't interest us. But to the extent that they're investigating the same things, one can ask whether they would make the same discoveries. And of course they will! They would find the same laws as we do. Look, the inverse square law of gravitation which Newton discovered here on Earth is simply a fact of nature, it's universal. That fact would also be discovered by physicists on Mars or in the Andromeda galaxy or wherever.

**Phillip:**

And yet there do seem to be suggestions that there are at least ethnic variations regarding ability to do science.

**Paul:**

Ah, but that's total nonsense!

**Phillip:**

But it's not. We recognise that the Chinese, for example, are doing wonderfully in physics, the Japanese less so.

**Paul:**

Again, you must distinguish between science and its practitioners. Look at the way that the Jews from Europe dominated physics for 50 years. There must be something about their education system, their culture — I don't know

SCIENCE AND TRUTH

what it is; it is interesting to speculate. We can all recognise that certain groups tend to dominate certain subjects. Today one thinks of the Chinese in physics, and I have no doubt that in other disciplines other national or ethnic groups also have a strong presence. There may well be cultural reasons why people in those ethnic groups go into certain disciplines in the first place, and are good at them. However, that doesn't mean the science is good only for their particular culture. The whole point about science is that it belongs to everybody. It's pancultural. If a particular ethnic group happens to make certain discoveries, then we can all check those discoveries for ourselves. That is the essence of science: it is in the public domain so that everyone can test it and agree on it. Science is objective knowledge. It is the most reliable type of knowledge we have.

**Phillip:**

Okay, you have raised the issue of its reliability. Well, another criticism frequently made, though often not very eloquently expressed, is that science is simply another way of looking at what we call reality, and by no means the superior way. You would argue, of course, that science is the ultimate, the most reliable, method.

**Paul:**

I do think that scientific knowledge is the most reliable

## MORE BIG QUESTIONS

form of knowledge we have about the natural world. Where it is superior to other systems of thought, like magic, religion, folklore, ancient wisdom and so forth, is in leading us to discover things we would never find out in any other way. Let me give you a striking example. Neutrinos are subatomic particles the effects of which people never notice in daily life because neutrinos are so elusive. In fact, it has been computed that the average neutrino interacts with ordinary matter so weakly that it could go through about 50 light years of solid lead without being stopped! You need very sophisticated scientific instrumentation to discover that these things really exist, and yet they're everywhere. It turns out that neutrinos are easily the most common objects in the universe. There are about a billion neutrinos for every other particle. If you glance at the sun, which is a nearby source of neutrinos, more of them pass through the pupil of your eye in one second than there are people on this planet. So these neutrinos are going through us the whole time, trillions upon trillions of neutrinos, and we just don't notice it. In fact, the entire universe is a sea of neutrinos, and ordinary matter of the sort that you and I are made of is just a tiny impurity in this vast ocean.

Now you might think that neutrinos are of no particular significance given that they are so elusive, but it so happens that they have an important role to play in life. Life as we know it is based on the element carbon, and carbon

## SCIENCE AND TRUTH

wasn't present in the early universe right after the big bang. Almost all of it has been manufactured inside stars by nuclear fusion. It turns out that if it weren't for neutrinos, the carbon would still be in those stars. The reason is that processes involving neutrinos which occur in the cores of some heavy stars make them explode. These so-called supernovae spew the stellar material, laced with life-giving carbon, around the galaxy. Some of this material gets incorporated into new generations of stars and planets, and perhaps ultimately into a biosphere. Earth's vital carbon started out in the cores of ancient stars, and it became available for life on Earth only by virtue of exotic neutrino processes. So neutrinos really do make a difference! Yet if it weren't for science we would never know they were there.

**Phillip:**

Another criticism that is made of science is that it has introduced 'megadeath' and 'overkill' to the human vocabulary. We look back on a century of a 160 million dead from warfare, and a lot of these deaths are attributed to the products of science — Hiroshima and Nagasaki, for example, and perhaps the fact that we have been having the third world war in instalments. To what extent is science guilty?

**Paul:**

Science is knowledge, and knowledge is power. And power

## MORE BIG QUESTIONS

can be used for good or evil. It's entirely in the hands of the people who use the fruits of science. If you look back at the horrors of the twentieth century, at the weapons of mass destruction, at industrial pollution and so forth, then of course these offences have been exacerbated by the fruits of science. We can now do the horrible things that people were doing a long time ago, only on a grander scale. But this isn't a sin confined to the twentieth century. I like to take the example of fire, a very ancient discovery. Fire can be used for good or evil, too. You can cook with fire or you can burn down somebody's village. You can clear land for agriculture or you can destroy a rainforest. Even the strongest opponents of science do not suggest that we ban fire! Society as a whole must decide how scientific developments are to be used.

**Phillip:**

You're offering a splendid vision of democracy, but in this voting system the scientist's vote seems to count for more. The scientist gets a bigger vote.

**Paul:**

I don't think that scientists get a bigger vote at all. In fact, a lot of people feel that scientists should be kept out of the debate altogether. The emphasis seems to be on restricting what scientists might do, rather than involving them in the discussion about what is good and bad.

SCIENCE AND TRUTH

**Phillip:**

Paul, you argue, and no-one can dispute it, that science is the most powerful tool available to us, but are there others of quality?

**Paul:**

I don't think that science is terribly good at informing us about ethics, about choices we have to make in society of a social or political nature. People often ask me at public lectures: 'You're a physicist. You understand about forces in the universe. What about forces for good and forces for evil'. I usually respond by saying: 'Well, you don't go to a physicist to ask about good and evil!' Naturally I have my personal opinions about what's right and wrong, but they are no better or worse than yours. Being a scientist doesn't especially qualify me to pronounce on matters of ethics or social policy.

**Phillip:**

But Paul, people *do* go to physicists, increasingly, for comments on good and evil. In fact, one other criticism of science is that the physicist has become, in more than one sense of the term, the new priest.

**Paul:**

Yes, I believe that is so, perhaps because people are awed by the power of science and therefore they expect science

25

MORE BIG QUESTIONS

to provide the answers to everything. They are also impressed by the way in which the frontiers of science are touching on those age-old questions of existence like 'How did the universe begin?', 'How did life begin?', 'What is the nature of consciousness?', 'How will it all end?' and so on. These are areas that were once exclusively the province of religion and philosophy. Now science is tangling with them and, furthermore, the scientists seem to be coming up with answers. All this may create the false impression that scientists know about everything. They don't.

**Phillip:**

I'm glad you're sceptical, because the other great criticism that's made of science is of its hubris. There's been a lot of glib talk in recent years that at any moment now someone at Princeton, Yale, Harvard, Oxford or wherever is going to jot up on the blackboard an equation which will be the 'Theory of Everything'. This sort of arrogance does seem to be producing hostility.

**Paul:**

Well, Phillip, I don't have any difficulty with the idea of a so-called Theory of Everything. I think that there might well be one just around the corner. But we come back to the point raised earlier — reductionism. When physicists refer to a Theory of Everything, it's in a purely reductionistic

SCIENCE AND TRUTH

sense. Nobody claims it would be the end of science, the whole story. It pretends only to be the culmination of the reductionist's programme. Let me explain. It may well be that we can identify the basic units, the fundamental entities, out of which the material world is built. Whether they turn out to be particles or little bits of string or something else we haven't thought of yet is irrelevant. If there are these basic entities underlying everything, and if there's a simple set of laws that connects them — and I hope and expect that there is — then we might well be able to write down a mathematical formula that would capture all of reality at that fundamental level. Nevertheless, it would be wrong to suppose that that is everything there is. A lot would be left out of such a description of nature. It wouldn't tell us about everyday things like why you choose coffee rather than tea to drink in the afternoon, for example.

Phillip:

Another thing which makes science look suspiciously like religion is the attitude to it of people such as me. I've spent years talking to you on various topics, and I grope to understand, but I accept as an article of faith — me, an atheist — that science is getting it right. This makes me very little different from someone who wandered into a vast fourteenth- or fifteenth-century cathedral and believed what was being said from the pulpit. Do you recognise that this is a problem?

## MORE BIG QUESTIONS

### Paul:

It certainly is a problem when scientists are occasionally treated like high priests of some latter-day religion. And some scientists play the part, declaiming as if they had a hot line to God. All I'm saying is that scientific knowledge is reliable knowledge, but scientists are not infallible! Scientific knowledge is always tentative, always provisional. The strength of science lies in the way that its theories are put up for falsification, and are continually being modified. A scientific theory is not accepted until it has been battle-tested by a sceptical scientific community. That is the essential feature that makes science different from religion. It's not a matter of just taking on faith the pronouncements of some particular scientist. There are always rivals in the scientific community who would just love to prove that scientist wrong. For example, there are people testing Einstein's theory of relativity the whole time, testing it at the fundamental level, trying to find something wrong with it. That is a very healthy state of affairs. The scientist comes up with a theory and everyone tries to shoot it down. If they fail to shoot it down after a lot of effort, then one can fairly conclude that the theory is a rather reliable description of the world. But nobody suggests it is the last word on the subject.

### Phillip:

You raise the subject of science and religion. It is interesting

SCIENCE AND TRUTH

that science, arguably, began with priests and then, of course, two parallel explorations of reality persisted for centuries. There is now, it would seem, the possibility of a convergence. Indeed you, as winner of the 1995 Templeton Prize for Progress in Religion, to some extent embody this convergence. You are a scientist, and yet you have been awarded a prize for your contributions to theology. Do you see science and religion converging?

Paul:

You are quite right that theology was the midwife of science. Again this is a matter of historical fact. That's no surprise because the Christian religion that dominated Europe in the seventeenth century had a long tradition of scholarly enquiry. Theologians such as Augustine and Thomas Aquinas set out their thinking in a rational and rigorous way. They formulated very deep ideas about physical existence, about nature and the order in nature, about creation and about God, and God's qualities, and so on. They constructed a sort of systematic theology, much like the Greeks constructed a systematic geometry. It was from this tradition that early scientists like Newton and Kepler began their investigations of nature, applying the sorts of principles and the type of reasoning to the natural world that theologians had already developed. As a result they made all kinds of discoveries that would never have emerged from alternative modes of

## MORE BIG QUESTIONS

investigation like mysticism and shamanism. Science grew out of that particular monotheistic way of thinking about the world. Even today, scientists unwittingly adopt a theological world view. For example, it is essential that a scientist believes that there is a law-like order in nature which is at least partially intelligible to human beings. If you didn't believe that then you couldn't be a scientist. You simply couldn't do science if you didn't think the world was both ordered and intelligible. But that's essentially a theological position. So I find it no surprise, now that science has matured over three or four hundred years, that it has begun to rediscover it's theological roots. Armed with their new knowledge, scientists have begun to return, in a very serious way, to those ancient questions of existence, questions like the ultimate origin of things. And they are getting some answers!

No wonder that people who have been drawn to ask those theological questions are increasingly turning to scientists for the answers. I therefore find this a very natural convergence. However, there is also a somewhat artificial bringing together of these two strands of thought in a way that I regard as wholly inappropriate. I am referring to cases where this or that religious group starts out by already deciding what they believe in advance, and then plunder science to bolster those beliefs. The whole point about science is it takes place in the spirit of openness. Individual

## SCIENCE AND TRUTH

scientists might think it would be nice if such-and-such were the case, but they have to be totally open-minded and accept the fact that if the evidence contradicts their pet theory then they should change their mind. It's no good saying, 'Well I already know that God did this and God did that — the world was created in seven days or something — and I'm going to find something in science that will support it.' That is a travesty of science. The point about scientific method is that first you see what the science tells us and then you draw your theological conclusions from it. You mustn't go backwards.

**Phillip:**

As I remarked at the beginning, a century of scientific triumph. We also leave a century which is bedevilled by what Isaac Asimov would describe as 'the armies of the night'. We see the rise of fundamentalism in all the major religious groupings. We see the nonsense of the 'New Age'. We see an upsurge in mediaeval superstitions. How can this happen? How can we have these parallel universes?

**Paul:**

Yes, I sometimes wonder what it is about the late twentieth century that has given rise to all these sorts of fringe beliefs or fringe elements. Most people have embraced science, and yet they still dabble in all kinds of nonsensical beliefs.

MORE BIG QUESTIONS

I get deluged with manuscripts from people who are very happy to quote this or that law of physics in support of their idea of, say, a perpetual motion machine. When you point out that their invention conflicts with the second law of thermodynamics, well, they don't like *that* law, but they'll accept the law of conservation of energy — that's okay! There is this widespread assumption that scientific knowledge, this huge corpus, is like a miraculous jar that you can dip into to pull out the bits that you like. I have a feeling that the scientific world view is struggling, it's losing the battle against the forces of emotionalism. I'm terribly concerned that we're going to return to a new Dark Age of ignorance and superstition.

## SELECTED READING

Jeremy Bernstein, *Cranks, Quarks and the Cosmos*, Basic Books, New York, 1978.

Paul Gross and Norman Levitt, *Higher Superstitions*, Johns Hopkins University Press, Baltimore, 1994.

Milton Rothman, *A Physicist's Guide to Skepticism*, Prometheus Books, Buffalo, NY, 1988.

Michael Shermer, *Why People Believe Weird Things*, Macmillan, London, 1997.

Steven Weinberg, *Dreams of a Final Theory*, Pantheon, New York, 1992.

Margaret Wertheim, *Pythagoras' Trousers: God, physics and the gender wars*, Fourth Estate, London, 1996.

John Ziman, *Reliable Knowledge*, Cambridge University Press, Cambridge, 1988.

TWO

# IN SEARCH OF EDEN

**Phillip:**

In Egyptian mythology, Ra stands on the primordial hill, shaped like a pyramid, and masturbates. And from his semen is created all life. In other cultures, it's an earth mother, a goddess who brings life into being. Every culture has its story — a rainbow serpent, a deity creating man out of dust. It's perhaps the biggest of the big questions — the origins of life. Now science has its own version of Genesis. But is it any more credible than the ancient mythologies?

**Paul:**

First, I should like to say that the scientific attempt to explain the origin of life proceeds from the assumption that whatever it was that happened was a natural process: no miracles, no supernatural intervention. It was by ordinary atoms doing extraordinary things that life was brought into existence. Scientists have to start with that assumption. The biggest problem is that life on Earth may well have originated with a unique event, perhaps unique on Earth, perhaps even unique in the entire universe. If it only

MORE BIG QUESTIONS

happened once, then science will have a lot of difficulty in reconstructing the precise details, because it's not just a matter of chemistry, geology, astronomy and so on — it's also a matter of history. There may have been a unique historical sequence of processes that spawned life that simply cannot, or could not, be reproduced elsewhere.

**Phillip:**

But given scientific hubris, that's not going to stop science, is it?

**Paul:**

Exactly right. Scientists feel that even if they don't know the precise details of what happened, they could at least work out the general process. We might be able to determine, for example, whether the transition from a non-living chemical mixture to life is something that is quite likely, under suitable circumstances, or extremely unlikely. That's really the question we'd like to answer because the issue as to whether we're alone in the universe, or whether it's teeming with life, hinges on how easy it is for life to emerge given suitable conditions.

**Phillip:**

Is there anything in the genetic record which suggests any sort of life force?

## IN SEARCH OF EDEN

**Paul:**

No, there is not. In fact, the concept of a life force has been completely discredited. It's a very unhelpful notion. It's also a very ancient one, I might say, going back at least to Plato. Both he and Aristotle had the idea that everything has a sort of immaterial soul that animates it. The Bible mentions 'breath' as the key factor that bestows life. We still talk about breathing life into something. Then, in the Middle Ages, the life force was associated with blood. Again, people still refer to 'the life blood'. After that it got a bit more scientific.

When electricity was discovered, that seemed a mysterious sort of thing, and so people conjectured that maybe it was the elusive life force. Remember Volta's experiments with the frogs' legs? He removed the muscle, wired it up to a battery and found that a pulse of electricity made the muscle twitch. You could almost believe it was bringing it to life again. In Mary Shelley's story *Frankenstein*, the monster was brought to life by a great bolt of electricity. Eventually it was discovered that electricity was actually a pretty straightforward phenomenon, and so ideas about what the life force might be moved on again.

In the late nineteenth century, physicists believed that all of space was filled with an invisible medium called the aether. Some people suggested that maybe this mysterious substance was somehow connected with life. Spiritualists

## MORE BIG QUESTIONS

began to talk of one's 'aetheric body' that survives death. In fact, they still do! Alas, Einstein's theory of relativity did away with the aether, and experiments failed to find any trace of it. But there was no lack of other strange physical concepts to appeal to in the search for the life force. Even radioactivity was suggested: there was a time when people thought that if you irradiated something with radium you might vivify it.

All of these ideas have been completely discredited. They are total rubbish. The fall-back position which some people then took was to suggest that the life force is confined to life itself, a special sort of essence. But such ideas achieve nothing because if all the life force does is to explain life then the argument becomes circular. To claim that the life force manifests itself only in a living organism doesn't explain anything; it just says that things are living because they are alive. So I don't think we need to invoke the life force. Moreover, when you look at living organisms at the level of individual atoms and molecules, what you find is that they are subject to perfectly ordinary forces, like electromagnetism. They obey the normal laws of physics and chemistry. There is no evidence that an atom of, say, carbon acquires a special 'zing' by its incorporation in a living cell. We don't need any extra force or invisible guiding hand to explain what the atoms of a living thing are doing.

### IN SEARCH OF EDEN

**Phillip:**

It might be useful to put the origin of life into a time scale. When did the whole process begin? About four billion years ago?

**Paul:**

As yet we don't know exactly when life began on Earth, but there are fossils right here in Australia that have been dated at 3.5 billion years. For comparison, the Earth itself has been dated using radioactivity measurements at 4.5 billion years old, so life has existed here for a large fraction of the lifetime of the planet. There is a hint of life even earlier than the Australian findings in rocks from Greenland, suggesting that life may have been making its mark 3.8 billion years ago.

**Phillip:**

What do you mean a hint of life?

**Paul:**

Life does more than just leave blob-like fossils in rocks. It can change the chemistry of the rocks, too. In particular, if you study the different isotopes of carbon trapped in these rocks from Greenland, there's a suggestion that they have been changed in their relative abundances. The natural environment contains two stable isotopes of carbon with slightly different masses. Organisms prefer to use the lighter

## MORE BIG QUESTIONS

isotope, and so biological processes have the effect of concentrating it at the expense of the heavier isotope.

**Phillip:**

Can you tell us about the so-called 'heavy bombardment', because it seems to coincide with the earliest fossil record of life?

**Paul:**

Astronomers think that the solar system began when a large cloud of mainly hydrogen gas left over from the big bang shrank under its own weight and, spinning ever faster, at its centre formed a glowing mass which eventually became the sun. This was surrounded by a residual disc of swirling debris, consisting of gas and dust, which aggregated to form the planets. The Earth was one of these aggregations. But of course the planets didn't form overnight, it was an extended process, and in particular a lot of the debris that was flying around hit the newly-formed solid bodies, sometimes with great violence. Indeed, even today rocks crash into the earth from time to time; we call them meteorites. In the early days this bombardment would have been very intense. You need only look at the moon, which is pockmarked with millions of craters, a mute testimony to the ferocity of the early bombardment phase. Earth, too, has impact craters, but most have eroded away.

**Phillip:**

And it's not just holes is it? It's new material that then patinates the planet.

**Paul:**

That's exactly right. The young Earth was accreting — accumulating — material from comets, asteroids, and dwarf planets from farther out in the solar system. They brought to the Earth water and life-encouraging organic molecules that would eventually be incorporated into the biosphere.

**Phillip:**

But crucial though the bombardment was for the delivery of the raw materials of life, it must also have presented a major hazard. It would seem to be an incredibly hostile time for life to be beginning, during such a bombardment.

**Paul:**

Yes, it wouldn't have been good to be around when there were huge objects up to 100 kilometres across crashing down out of the sky. If the Earth were hit today by a 10 kilometre-sized object, the global pollution of dust and acid rain would probably destroy the majority of species on the planet. And such cataclysms do happen from time to time. Every 10 to 100 million years or so, the Earth takes a hit from an object of that sort of size. It is well known that the

MORE BIG QUESTIONS

dinosaurs were most likely wiped out by a cosmic catastrophe of this sort, along with many other species.

Phillip:
Paul, have you got the time on you at the moment?

Paul:
We don't know when it's going to happen! It's a more-or-less random process, you see, so you cannot predict the next big impact. What does seem certain is that during the first 700 million years of the Earth's history this cosmic bombardment would have been much more intense and the size of the impacting bodies much larger. The effect of an impact by a very large object, say 100 kilometres across, is quite awesome. The object itself would be mainly vaporised. The blast would displace the Earth's atmosphere, boil its oceans and create a rock vapour atmosphere that would envelop the planet and glow to a temperature of about 3000 degrees, thoroughly sterilising the surface. If there had been any life on the Earth's surface prior to about 3.8 billion years ago it wouldn't have lasted very long following one of these impacts!

Phillip:
So we have a hint of life prior to the end of the heavy early bombardment, or at any rate coinciding with its end.

In Search of Eden

It seems that life got going fairly rapidly once the pounding tailed off.

Paul:

Yes, it is something of a puzzle that life got started so soon after the heavy bombardment ceased. It suggests either that life will emerge pretty quickly under favourable circumstances, or else that it came to Earth from outer space, pre-formed.

Phillip:

Fred Hoyle, the British theoretical astronomer and opponent of big bang theory, used to argue that life might have been blown around the universe with comets. Is there any possibility in this? Is it useful even to think about life being introduced to Earth in this way?

Paul:

It is certainly true that life could have come to Earth from somewhere else in the universe. I'll have more to say on that topic in the next chapter. However, it doesn't solve the problem of the origin of life. All it does is to push it off into space. It was very fashionable in the nineteenth century to suppose that the universe didn't have an origin. If that was correct, one could ask, therefore, why does life have to have an origin? If life can jump from place to place, we could imagine a universe in which life has always existed

## MORE BIG QUESTIONS

and the universe has always existed. Some people are content with that. They think it somehow explains life, but of course it doesn't. You don't explain something by supposing it has always been there.

**Phillip:**

Isn't there evidence within the genetic code contained in all forms of life that there was a sort of Eden moment — a moment when life just began?

**Paul:**

It's certainly the case that all known forms of life on Earth seem to have a single common ancestor, for reasons I shall come to shortly. I am not talking about a common ancestor just for you and me, but also for the mushrooms out on the lawn, the kangaroos hopping about in the bush, and even bacteria. We all seem to go back to a single universal pre-cursor. Darwin had a neat metaphor to explain this, called the Tree of Life *(see Fig. 1)*. At the base is the trunk, which represents the first living thing. The trunk then splits into branches, and these in turn re-branch and re-branch until there are millions of different species. Most of them become extinct, but the twiglets at the top of the diagram represent the species that are alive today — the survivors. If you start out at any twig and trace a route back down the tree you will eventually get all the way down to the trunk. There will always be an earliest point of convergence where all existing living things have a common ancestor.

**Phillip:**
But that is different from the origin of life itself?

**Paul:**
Yes that's right. A lot of people are confused by this. The last common ancestor is not the same as the first living thing. I have denoted the universal ancestor of all extant life by a circle part way down the tree *(see Fig. 1)*. It is the highest point on the tree connected to all the twigs at the top. Notice that there are branches of the tree that sprout

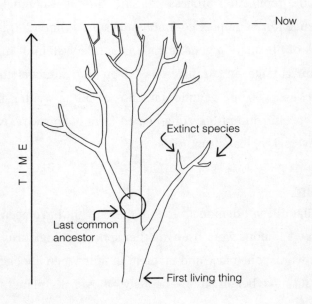

MORE BIG QUESTIONS

out from the trunk below this point. These represent species that became extinct and left no descendants. Almost certainly the last common ancestor was much more complex than the first living thing. We know that because all surviving life forms on Earth are immensely complicated in very specific ways, suggesting that the common ancestor was already a very complicated organism. If you look at living cells they have elaborate structures inside them, such as tiny factories called ribosomes used for making proteins. They have also got nucleic acids which are themselves very complicated molecules. Many of the proteins common to all extant life are highly specialised in their structure and function, especially the customised enzymes associated with the replication process. Perhaps the most compelling evidence for a complex common ancestor is that all known forms of life share a genetic code, a subtle system of information storage and transfer based on the numbers three and twenty. So the genetic database of life is written in a very specific and rather complicated form of software, with a universal logical structure.

Phillip:

But that doesn't demonstrate that there might have been, to borrow a famous word from another sphere, a singularity; in other words, one place and moment in time when life began. It could have begun simultaneously all over the planet.

**IN SEARCH OF EDEN**

Paul:

If it began like that, in many different places at once, we would expect to find many different life forms with different chemical structures and different logical systems. Instead, everything that we study shares a common physical structure, a common chemical system, a common genetic code. This implies that if life did spring into existence many times on the surface of the Earth, only one lot survived. In fact, there has been considerable discussion among scientists as to why that might have been. After all, if life is as easy to form as the fossil record suggests, then you would expect it to happen many times over. What has become of all these other life forms? Perhaps it was a case of only the toughest form being able to withstand the rigours of the bombardment — or maybe the survivors ate the rest. We simply don't know.

Phillip:

Can laboratory experiments provide a clue? What happened in the 1950s when a couple of scientists attempted to replicate what they imagined were the primordial conditions?

Paul:

One way you can try and find out how life began is to simulate the conditions that the early Earth might have had. This was done in 1951 in a famous experiment at the University of Chicago by Harold Urey and his student Stanley

MORE BIG QUESTIONS

Miller. They took some methane, ammonia and hydrogen
— gases common in the outer planets and ones the experi-
mentors believed would have been part of the Earth's
primeval atmosphere — and put them in a flask along
with some water. Then they sparked electricity through
the mixture for a week or so to simulate lightning. They
chose to use electricity, but other sources, including sound
energy, have since been used to good effect.

Miller and Urey were delighted to find that the liquid
turned a sort of reddish-brown colour. When they analysed
it they found that it contained amino acids. Now amino
acids are very basic organic chemicals that are the building
blocks of proteins. Proteins are, of course, absolutely crucial
to life. So Miller and Urey felt that this was a wonderful first
step to creating life in a test tube. If after a week you have
made the building blocks of proteins maybe after a year you
will make something more elaborate, and after a million
years you might make a genuine living thing. Something
might actually crawl out of this red-brown soup!

**Phillip:**

Were they able to play God in the laboratory?

**Paul:**

In the intervening years the significance of the Miller–Urey
experiment has been re-evaluated. First of all I should point

IN SEARCH OF EDEN

out that the Earth's early atmosphere almost certainly didn't contain large amounts of the gases used in their experiment because these gases are generally too unstable so close to the sun, so there's a bit of a problem about that. But more to the point, there is a conceptual problem here. It's a mistake to suppose that there is a sort of road, with life as its destination, along which a chemical mixture is inexorably conveyed by the passage of time. It isn't just a matter of carrying on doing more of the same, with the amino acids obligingly assembling themselves into proteins and the proteins joining up with nucleic acids, and so on, to eventually make a living thing. It isn't a one-way street like that, and the reason is very basic. Making amino acids is what a physicist would call 'thermodynamically downhill', which means it is a natural process that occurs automatically, like crystallisation. But hooking the amino acids together into long chains to make proteins goes the other way. That is an 'uphill' — a statistically more difficult or unlikely — process.

Let me give you an analogy. It's a little bit like going for a walk in the countryside, coming across a pile of bricks and assuming that there will be a house around the corner. There is a big difference between a pile of bricks and a house. Now part of the problem here is that attaching the amino acids together to make proteins costs energy. True, there was no lack of energy on the young Earth, but the problem is not energy *per se*. Rather, it is how this energy *organised* itself in such a way as to produce this extremely elaborate thing called a protein.

**Phillip:**
Okay, solve the problem for us.

**Paul:**
Some scientists say, just throw energy at it and it will happen spontaneously. That is a little bit like saying: put a stick of dynamite under the pile of bricks, and *bang*, you've got a house! Of course you won't have a house, you'll just have a mess. The difficulty in trying to explain the origin of life is in accounting for how the elaborate organisational structure of these complex molecules came into existence spontaneously from a random input of energy. How did these very specific complex molecules assemble themselves?

**Phillip:**
Does this suggest lots of sticks of dynamite under lots of piles of bricks?

**Paul:**
That's one game you can play. You can say that if you replay the scenario often enough on enough planets, and you wait long enough, sooner or later, just by chance, the

## IN SEARCH OF EDEN

right molecular combination will occur. The argument is absolutely correct. Chance will work miracles given enough time. However, when you put the numbers in you find, to your absolute horror, that you could wait almost forever just to get a single protein. The odds of shuffling amino acids at random into just one short protein are one in $10^{130}$ — that's a one followed by 130 zeros!

**Phillip:**

Paul, I'm getting very depressed by this because it sounds like life is never going to happen. For heaven's sake do something!

**Paul:**

If you're going to do it just by random shuffling you would wait almost forever, so I don't think that is the answer. When I give public lectures and talk about the universe and all the stars and planets and so on, someone from the audience will often comment at the end: 'The universe is so vast, there are so many stars out there, so many planets, it would be absurd to suppose that we are alone. There must be life on one of those planets somewhere.' But that is simply not true! The reasoning is wrong. When you look at the numbers we have just been talking about it is clearly a logical fallacy to suppose that just because you have a huge number of planets you are necessarily going to produce life

MORE BIG QUESTIONS

somewhere else. The total number of planets that are likely to exist within our observable universe has been estimated at about $10^{20}$, that is a one followed by twenty zeros. And we were just talking about 1 followed by 130 zeros, and that is for a single protein! Twenty powers of ten doesn't make much of a dent in 130. It clearly is not going to help very much just extending the space to the observable universe. The mathematics is clear: the odds against making life by some sort of random molecular shuffling anywhere in the observable universe are infinitesimal. So I don't think that random shuffling explains how it happened.

**Phillip:**

If something doesn't happen soon, are we going to de-materialise?

**Paul:**

Don't worry, there are other ways of approaching this problem. One possibility is that life is somehow written into the basic laws of the universe. What this means is that the laws of the universe are curiously bio-friendly — they have been rigged in favour of producing certain types of complex structures that are biologically relevant. In other words, you put all these simple molecules into a chemical mix, a soup if you like, and you let it do its stuff. The molecules mill around, engaging in lots of different reactions,

IN SEARCH OF EDEN

but somehow the laws of chemistry favour the production of just those chemical substances that are needed for life. In other words life is brought into being because essential molecules such as proteins form more readily than others. So this argues that there is a built-in bias in nature's laws.

**Phillip:**

That would suggest that life would not only spontaneously combust around the planet, but around the universe.

**Paul:**

Yes, it would happen almost everywhere that you looked for it. A lot of people believe this theory, but I think that it implies a sort of cosmic conspiracy of gigantic proportions because it means that the underlying laws of physics and chemistry somehow 'know' about something as complex as a life form.

**Phillip:**

That almost sounds like the life force.

**Paul:**

It does indeed sound very mystical. It implies that the existence of life is written somewhere deep down in the basic workings of the universe. For a physicist the problem with this idea is that the laws of physics — and the laws of

MORE BIG QUESTIONS

chemistry that follow from them — are simple, mathematical and general. By contrast, life is complex, non-mathematical and very, very specific. The difficulty is to understand how in a law-like way life can follow from the primordial soup with the sort of reliability and dependability that many scientists claim. I don't think that this is the answer either. It's too contrived.

The third possibility is that life arises as a result of what is often called self-organisation. That is to say that under certain circumstances, matter and energy have an uncanny ability to organise themselves into more and more complex structures, although not directed towards life — not with life as a fixed goal or end product.

**Phillip:**

Not a *canny* ability in other words.

**Paul:**

No, but the increase in complexity that arises from some self-organising physical and chemical processes can be quite surprising. We see this in many areas of investigation. You don't have to study living organisms to see self-generated complexity. There are examples all around us.

**Phillip:**

In crystals, for example.

52

**Paul:**

Take a snowflake. A snowflake is an ordered complex pattern, but there is no gene for a snowflake; there is no mystical force at work, no 'snowflake' destiny written into the laws of physics, and yet snowflakes form spontaneously and can become very elaborate. So there *are* examples where physical forces and laws conspire to produce elaborate, organised, complex systems, and we might suppose that in the right conditions there will be a hierarchy of complexity, a self-generating or bootstrapping effect, where chemicals organise themselves to form one level of complexity, and then the next, and then the next, and so on. It goes on and on and on, until something truly living emerges.

But, the truth of the matter is we absolutely don't know. We don't know how life began. I think we know roughly where and when. But we still don't know how.

**Phillip:**

Whatever chemical magic may have happened, life presupposes some sort of information system, doesn't it?

**Paul:**

Yes, it does. I think that is the essential point. The problem about life is not what we are made of — the hardware — it's the information content, the software. It is the software that makes us living; the biological information contained in us.

**Phillip:**

But you reject the notion of that software being a life force.

**Paul:**

Absolutely, though to be fair, it does have some elements of the life force in as much as it is non-material. Software, or information, is, by its very nature, something that can be encoded in hardware, but which enjoys a kind of independent existence itself. But otherwise it is really quite different from the idea of a life force because I'm not talking about any sort of magical or mystical extra essence. Information is a familiar concept.

In my opinion, the great mystery about the origin of life is where the biological information came from in the first place. That is the crux of the matter, not the complicated chemistry and how it came into being. We won't find the secret of life in the laws of chemistry. The biological information must have come from our environment, of course, but how did it concentrate, how did it go on accumulating, in molecules, to the extent that we would call them living?

**Phillip:**

Paul, I'm computer illiterate. I wonder if you could find another metaphor for the information system other than software/hardware.

## IN SEARCH OF EDEN

**Paul:**

There is one that I like quite a lot, which is a comparison between flying a kite and flying a radio-controlled plane. A kite is literally hardwired to the controller on the ground. By contrast, a radio-controlled plane has an informational channel. How does the plane perform its aerobatics? You push and pull some levers, and these signals are encoded into electromagnetic pulses. That information is then sent up to the plane and decoded. Note that the radio waves themselves don't push and pull the plane around. The signals encoded in the radio waves merely harness other forces and liberate them to do the job. So the radio channel plays the role of an informational channel rather than a physical push–pull link.

What has all this to do with life? As we know it, life is based on a kind of deal struck between two very different classes of molecules. One of these are the nucleic acids, which contain the genetic information encoded in the sequence of their atoms. These molecules can't do very much. It is the proteins, the other class of molecules, that are the real workers in biology. But both types of molecules need the other: the nucleic acids on their own are helpless; the proteins on their own are also helpless.

**Phillip:**

This is chicken and egg stuff, isn't it?

## MORE BIG QUESTIONS

**Paul:**

Precisely. This is the ultimate chicken-and-egg problem. The great mystery about the origin of life is, which came first: chicken or egg? Was it the nucleic acids or the proteins? That is the traditional biochemical mystery. But I think the ultimate mystery of the origin of life is not so much how did two sets of complicated inter-dependent molecules ever arise spontaneously and get together, but more 'what was it that turned the kite into the radio-controlled plane'? Because however much you evolve a kite, it ain't going to be a radio-controlled plane. The reason is, of course, that the notion of radio control employing a coded informational channel is a totally different kind of conceptual scheme from the kite. It is not just a matter of more of the same, but something totally new. So, in my opinion, the real mystery of the origin of life is how did a system leap that gap from being mere hardware, like the hard-wired kite, to being a software-mediated chicken-and-egg combination?

**Phillip:**

Is there any place on, or in, the Earth today which might be closer to what things were like at the beginning, to give us a clue about the earliest life forms?

**Paul:**

It turns out that there is. If you go deep down under the

## IN SEARCH OF EDEN

ground or under the ocean, particularly close to volcanic vents, then you do indeed find in localised pockets a large amount of the types of gases, such as methane and hydrogen, that Miller and Urey used in their experiment, coming up out of the Earth's crust. And the extraordinary thing is, if you drill down into the hot rock, you find that there are organisms living deep down there even today. These microbes are making a living, not in the atmosphere, and not by utilising sunlight or eating other organisms, but directly from the chemicals and heat energy coming up out of the crust. In other words, they are effectively living off the rocks beneath our feet, or beneath the sea.

**Phillip:**

Could these deep locations have provided, in effect, bomb shelters during the bombardment?

**Paul:**

Some scientists have suggested this. They think that during the time of heavy bombardment, when the surface of the Earth was sterilised by impacts, there could still have been a comfy niche deep underground. Pulses of heat from the major impacts might have travelled down perhaps a kilometre into the rock, but any microbes living deeper than that — if their comfort zone extended that far — would have been safe from this terrible bombardment. So maybe we have been looking at the wrong place all this time. Perhaps life didn't begin on the surface of the Earth in a 'warm little pond' as Darwin originally conjectured. Maybe life began instead in the region that has been traditionally associated with hell — the sulfurous volcanic depths, at intense temperatures and pressures — and came to the surface only later when it was safe to put its head up, when the bombardment ceased. In other words, perhaps life started hot and deep and only later migrated to the surface.

There is some interesting confirmation of this theory. If you study the genes of the micro-organisms that now live deep under the ground, or on the seabed in the dark near the ocean vents, you can tell something about the way in which they have evolved over time. It turns out that the least evolved organisms we know are those that live in these pressure cooker conditions, near the boiling vents. We can think of these microbes as like living fossils, left over from a time over 3.8 billion years ago when the Earth was a very different kind of place, and life had maybe just got started.

**Phillip:**

And are these strange microbes genetically connected to us?

**Paul:**

Yes, they are! In spite of their bizarre nature, these organisms still share with us the same genetic code, the same basic

## IN SEARCH OF EDEN

chemical structure. So it could be that when we study the microbes extracted from these hellish conditions we are looking at something very much like an ancient ancestor of you and me!

## SUGGESTED READING

A. G. Cairns-Smith, *Seven Clues to the Origin of Life*, Cambridge University Press, 1985.

Francis Crick and Leslie Orgel, *Life Itself: Its Nature and Origin*, Simon & Schuster, New York, 1981.

Paul Davies, *The Fifth Miracle*, Viking, Melbourne, 1998.

Christian de Duve, *Vital Dust*, Basic Books, New York, 1995.

Freeman Dyson, *Origins of Life*, Cambridge University Press, Cambridge, 1985.

Manfred Eigen, *Steps Towards Life* (trans. P. Woolley), Oxford University Press, Oxford, 1992.

Jacques Monod, *Chance and Necessity* (trans. A. Wainhouse), Knopf, New York, 1971.

Andrew Scott, *The Creation of Life*, Blackwell, Oxford, 1986.

Robert Shapiro, *Origins: A skeptic's guide to the creation of life on Earth*, Summit Books, New York, 1986.

THREE

# ARE WE ALONE IN THE UNIVERSE?

**Phillip:**

Human language is daunted by the scale of the cosmic enterprise. Words fail us when we gaze up at the stars and try to contemplate their significance — and our insignificance. But there is a word that I'm fond of, one that attempts to describe the feelings of awe, wonderment, curiosity and dread that fills us when we look up into the skies on a clear night. The word is 'numinous'. And with the feeling of the numinous comes another big question. Are we alone? Are there other forms of life — particularly of conscious life — out there? Should we attempt to make contact? How might this be possible? On the one hand, we acknowledge that the right conditions to kindle life might be so rare, so fugitive, that we're doomed to cosmic solitude. On the other hand, we're dealing with such immense numbers of suns and, presumably, of planets, that life forms may be as bountiful in the cosmos as they are on Earth. After all, in the observable universe there are $10^{20}$ — 100 billion billion — suns.

## ARE WE ALONE IN THE UNIVERSE?

**Paul:**

That's a lot, isn't it, a big number. Unfortunately not so big that if life formed as a result of an accidental shuffling of molecules — that is, if life *is* a chemical fluke — then it would be bound to occur twice.

**Phillip:**

But what if you add to those 100 billion billion suns the number of possible planets? You are then dealing with an even greater number.

**Paul:**

It's just another factor of ten or so. People are very bad at large number estimates. They think that a million is awfully big, and a billion just a bit bigger, and so on. Although 100 billion billion sounds like an enormous number, it is still absolutely tiny compared to the odds against forming life by random shuffling. It is undeniably true that the universe is vast: there are a huge number of stars and probably planets too. Nevertheless the odds against shuffling, say, amino acids into proteins, which we were talking about previously, are enormous — like one followed by 130 zeros as opposed to your puny number here of one followed by twenty zeros! A hundred billion billion doesn't begin to scratch the surface of the improbability of forming life, if it formed purely by accident. So if life is merely a chemical fluke, we

## More Big Questions

*are* alone. The only possibility of us *not* being alone is if there is something other than just a random shuffling process involved.

**Phillip:**

There are conflicting human emotions at work here. On the one hand, it is a very bleak thought, to suppose that we are alone in the universe. Many of us would like the company of user-friendly species from other galaxies. On the other hand, we have always been very arrogant; we rather like to think that we are at the centre of things.

**Paul:**

In some cultures, yes. But not all. The same argument was raging even in ancient Greece over 2000 years ago. The Greek atomists believed that we are not unique. They reasoned that the universe is nothing but indestructible particles moving in the void. This led them to conclude that extraterrestrial beings exist because if atoms can come together in certain combinations to form living things here on Earth, then they might do so on other worlds, too.

**Phillip:**

Does Christianity generally accept the notion that we are alone?

## ARE WE ALONE IN THE UNIVERSE?

**Paul:**

Christians have traditionally hated the idea that there could be intelligent life elsewhere. It causes all sorts of doctrinal difficulties for them. The problem is not so severe in other religions, but Christianity has particular difficulty, I think, with life elsewhere in the universe because Jesus Christ is traditionally held to be the Saviour of mankind only, which is hard on any alien beings whose ethical or spiritual stature might dwarf that of humans.

**Phillip:**

Let's reduce the scale from our 100 billion billion suns. Let's look at our own sun and one of our neighbouring planets — Mars. There has been a lot of speculation about life on Mars recently.

**Paul:**

Yes, there has. Mars has always been at the forefront of speculation about life beyond Earth. Remember how 100 years ago Percival Lowell claimed he saw canals on the surface of Mars? He believed there were alien beings who built these structures to bring melt water from the poles to the parched equatorial regions of the planet. Then in the 1960s our spacecraft went to Mars and didn't find any canals, or any other signs of life. For a while it looked as if Mars was not only red, but dead too.

MORE BIG QUESTIONS

Phillip:

Of course, there are the pseudo-scientists who claim there is a giant face on Mars surrounded by pyramids.

Paul:

Yes, there is the famous 'face on Mars' too, but we're not taking that seriously! The two Viking spacecraft that NASA sent to Mars in the 1970s were specifically designed to search for life. They scooped up some topsoil, analysed it in little on-board laboratories, and didn't find any compelling evidence for life — even microbial life. In fact, the surface of Mars turned out to be a pretty dreadful place. It's exceedingly dry, and very cold — rarely above the melting point of water. On top of that, it is drenched in deadly ultraviolet radiation, and the soil is incredibly oxidising, which is very dangerous to life. All in all, the surface of Mars is extremely hostile to any form of life that we know.

Phillip:

But Paul, you have established that life occurred on Earth in extremely inhospitable circumstances.

Paul:

That is true, and there has been some speculation that Antarctica can reproduce conditions not very dissimilar to the surface of Mars. Remarkably, there are organisms that

## ARE WE ALONE IN THE UNIVERSE?

live in the dry valleys of Antarctica that I think *could* live on the surface of Mars even today, if only they could be shielded from the ultraviolet radiation. So, I agree, it is not obvious that the surface of Mars is *completely* hostile to life even today. But nevertheless, it's not a place you would want to be stranded — 'not the type of place to raise a kid', to paraphrase Elton John's 'Rocket Man'. I think the real reason why Mars looks promising from the point of view of life is that we know that in the past it was warm and wet. The photographs of the Martian terrain show unmistakable signs of river valleys, and there were times when there was so much water on the surface of Mars there may even have been an ocean. Going back about 3.8 billion years, to a time when we know that there was probably life here on Earth, Mars wasn't so very dissimilar from Earth. So, I think that although Mars doesn't look terribly friendly for life today, in the past it would have been a different story.

### Phillip:

Let me return to the matter of the bombardment where the Earth, our planet, was patinated by large amounts of rubble being attracted to it. One possibility is that life might have been introduced to Earth as part of that process. Given that rocks have been traded back and forth between the two planets, could perhaps Earth life have been transmitted to Mars?

## MORE BIG QUESTIONS

**Paul:**

In my mind there is no doubt that if material can travel between the two planets, then so can organisms. It is entirely possible that microbes can hitch a ride on a rock and make their way from Mars to Earth or visa versa. We know that Mars and Earth receive hits from time to time with enough force to splash material into space; at the moment this happens about every few million years or so, on average. The ejected debris will be scattered around the solar system, and some of it will inevitably be swept up by other planets.

**Phillip:**

So, Paul, all things considered, do you think that there was life on Mars?

**Paul:**

I'm absolutely convinced that there was, in the remote past, if for no other reason than it would have got there from Earth along with the displaced rocks. The bombardment that took place in the early history of the solar system was so intense that it would have propelled an enormous number of rocks backwards and forwards between the two planets. We know that Mars was warm and wet at the time there was life on Earth, so I think it was inevitable that some Earth microbes would have made their way to Mars inside ejected rocks and found conditions there rather congenial.

## ARE WE ALONE IN THE UNIVERSE?

**Phillip:**

But would these little microbes piggybacking on pieces of rock have made it alive across that distance?

**Paul:**

I agree it does seem extraordinary that even a microbe could travel through inter-planetary space without being killed, but when you look at it carefully, it does appear to be possible. The first hazard is getting blasted off a planet by a major asteroid or comet impact event. While this looks unlikely, it actually turns out that an appreciable fraction of rocks can be flung into space by an impact without being unduly shocked or compressed. The Martian meteorites that we have here on Earth, for example, haven't been pulverised. I think a microbe could survive ejection from a planet. It could also survive the radiation in space because, cocooned inside the rock, it would be shielded from the worst of the ultraviolet radiation from the sun, and from the worst of the cosmic rays too. On arrival, a rock with a suitable trajectory could be braked by air friction and hit the ground at low speed without burning up. So, yes, I think a fraction of microbes could make it unscathed from one planet to another.

**Phillip:**

Conversely could life have begun on Mars and then been transferred here?

## MORE BIG QUESTIONS

**Paul:**

Absolutely. In fact, I think there is some reason to favour Mars over Earth for the origin of life. Mars is a smaller planet, so it would have had less of a bombardment problem. It would have been possible for microbes to live deeper in the Martian crust because it wasn't such a hot planet. Also, it is easier to blast stuff off Mars because of its lower gravity. So there is a chance that life began on Mars, maybe as early as 4, even 4.2, billion years ago, and was subsequently conveyed to Earth in some of the debris that was splashed off at a later stage. If that is correct, it leads to the bizarre conclusion that we are all descended from Martians!

**Phillip:**

How can we be sure that a rock on Earth had a Martian origin?

**Paul:**

Well, as it happens, the University of Adelaide has been in possession of a piece of Martian rock for decades, although nobody realised it until Dr Vic Gostin spotted its significance a few years ago. It is part of an object that fell in Egypt in 1911 near the town of Nakhla. Incidentally, it killed a dog. This is the only known example of a canine fatality caused by a cosmic object! To look at, this Martian meteorite is unremarkable. Frankly, it's little different from any old bit of rock that you might find in your garden.

### ARE WE ALONE IN THE UNIVERSE?

**Phillip:**

We established earlier that physicists, mathematicians and other members of your profession are regarded as high priests. I confessed to having a blind faith in your utterances, but I want you to *convince* me that there is rock on Earth that has come from Mars!

**Paul:**

You can't tell by looking at a rock that it has come from Mars — it is not red or anything. The first clue is that it is a type of rock called igneous, which means that it was produced by volcanic activity. Meteorites of the common-or-garden variety are all bits of debris left over from the formation of the solar system — primordial and largely unprocessed rocks that were not accumulated into planets. If something is made by a volcano, then there is only one place it can have originated, and that is a planet. So this rock must have come from a planet. Did it come from the Earth? Earth has volcanoes. No. How can we be sure? Because we have got a pretty good understanding of what Earth rocks are like. When you study the chemistry of this rock, you find that it is subtly different from any rocks on Earth. In particular, the oxygen isotopes in rocks from Mars have different ratios from Earth rocks and, incidentally, from moon rocks.

MORE BIG QUESTIONS

Phillip:

So it has a Martian fingerprint all over it.

Paul:

At least a non-terrestrial fingerprint. So, we are looking for a planet in the solar system, other than Earth or its moon, with volcanoes. Mars is the obvious answer. Look at the pictures of Mars — it has some of the biggest volcanoes in the solar system. It's a volcanic planet. However, even that is not the clincher. It turns out that the best evidence we have that meteorites come from Mars — and there are about a dozen of them that have been collected so far — is that trapped within the rock are gases from the Martian atmosphere. In the 1970s the Viking spacecraft, which landed on the surface of Mars, measured the different isotopes of the gases — argon, xenon and so on — in the thin Martian air. Those isotope ratios match exactly the isotope contents of our Martian rocks. That is just too much to be a coincidence, so they clearly do come from Mars. I don't think many scientists now seriously doubt that.

Phillip:

Do any of our Earth-bound meteorites contain hints of life?

Paul:

Yes, a meteorite found in Antarctica in 1984, code-named

## ARE WE ALONE IN THE UNIVERSE?

ALH84001, contains tantalising evidence for life. Indeed, there are some scientists at NASA who are convinced that life has been at work in that meteorite. There are three reasons why the NASA scientists are excited by it. One is that it contains tiny grains of carbonate — and to a geologist carbonate suggests one thing: water. Of course, all life as we know it depends on water. If you look very carefully with a microscope at these carbonate grains, there are other features, little mineral inclusions within them, which suggest that some sort of organic processing has gone on. If you saw such features in an Earth rock you would attribute them to bacterial activity.

**Phillip:**
It wouldn't be a line call? You would be absolutely confident that it was bacterial activity?

**Paul:**
It would be pretty certain if it was in an Earth rock, yes. But of course if you see it in a Mars rock, you think again. However, the mineral grains were not all. The scientists from NASA also found ring-shaped organic molecules known as PAHs which living organisms can produce. Unfortunately PAHs can also be made by normal chemical means, so it is not conclusive evidence for life. The third line of evidence, and I suppose the thing which most captured the public

**MORE BIG QUESTIONS**

attention when the results were announced, was the existence of tiny little sausage-shaped features, little microscopic blobs, reminiscent of fossilised bacteria. Nobody's claiming they are *living* bacteria, but they could be bacterial fossils. All these findings have been disputed — the jury is still out on them.

**Phillip:**

How old would these putative fossils be?

**Paul:**

The figure's a bit rubbery, but 3.6 billion years seems a good estimate. These could be very ancient Martian microbes.

**Phillip:**

And what prospects are there for life on Mars today?

**Paul:**

As we discussed earlier, the surface of Mars is not very promising for life. However, deep underground, where the permafrost is melted by geothermal heat, conditions may well resemble those beneath the surface of the Earth, a region we know is seething with microbial life. My personal belief is that there probably is microscopic life in the subsurface zone on Mars even today.

### ARE WE ALONE IN THE UNIVERSE?

**Phillip:**

Okay, let's take the optimistic view that yes, life did exist on Mars, and may even exist on Mars today. If that is the case we can extrapolate to the wider universe. The probability is that many of the billions of stars we have mentioned have planets. Do you take the view therefore, that life is likely to be bubbling away all over the cosmos?

**Paul:**

Because we are almost completely ignorant of how life began, that is an open question. Personally I would say that life is common throughout the universe, but I am arriving at that point of view largely on philosophical rather than scientific grounds.

**Phillip:**

Philosophical? In what sense?

**Paul:**

I don't believe that we are freaks, that life on Earth is the result of a single stupendous, meaningless accident. I think that life is part of the natural outworking of the underlying laws of physics, laws that govern a bio-friendly universe.

**Phillip:**

Is that an emotional need of yours?

MORE BIG QUESTIONS

## Paul:

Probably, yes. I'm coming at this entirely from the philosophical, or, if you like, emotional direction. Not from a scientific direction, because the scientific evidence is very equivocal. We don't know how life began. We have no idea whether it was a unique event or whether it is something that occurs easily under the right conditions. I might say that many scientists are biological determinists: they think that it is rather easy for life to form under the right conditions. They also point out the fact that the basic building blocks of life, the amino acids and so on, are very common throughout the universe, and that the stuff of which life is made — the basic elements like carbon, nitrogen, oxygen, hydrogen and so on — are among the most abundant elements in the universe. Therefore they conclude that life is likely to be abundant in the universe, but we don't know that. It is pure conjecture.

## Phillip:

If there is a miracle — and as an atheist I find that an embarrassing word to use — but if there is a miracle in the story of life, I find it in the growth or the development of consciousness: self-regarding, self-aware consciousness. Is there in your view a likelihood that consciousness would develop in other realms on other planets? Is that a part of the inevitability, the coding?

## ARE WE ALONE IN THE UNIVERSE?

**Paul:**

If we accept Darwin's theory of evolution as a complete picture of the evolutionary changes that have taken place among life on Earth, then it would seem extremely unlikely that consciousness would develop anywhere else. Consciousness would simply be a quirky little by-product of the blind groping of evolution, in the same way that fingernails and eyebrows and so on have appeared. In other words, they don't have any deep significance.

**Phillip:**

Some quirk.

**Paul:**

Naturally we regard it as immensely significant because we are the products of it. However, there is no known law that operates in evolution to direct the evolutionary change towards consciousness or intelligence. If evolution is blind, if it is just a random groping through the space of possibilities, then the chances of Earth's evolutionary pathway being paralleled on another planet are infinitesimal. Of course, if there is more to it than 'blind watchmaker' Darwinism, then this conclusion may be wrong. Consciousness and intelligence may emerge as a natural by-product of bio-friendly laws. We don't know, but it is important to put the matter to the test.

## MORE BIG QUESTIONS

**Phillip:**

By test, you mean SETI — the search for extraterrestrial intelligence — using radio telescopes to seek out signals from alien civilisations? Given your optimistic philosophy, do you regard SETI as a worthwhile project?

**Paul:**

When people ask me about SETI I say that it is almost certainly a hopeless enterprise, just because of the enormous odds against locating an alien intelligence even if the universe is full of them. Still, it's a glorious enterprise nonetheless, and well worth doing. I am a thorough supporter of SETI. Alas, though, the chances of success are extremely small.

**Phillip:**

Let's entertain a hypothesis, a mind game: Life abounds in the universe. Conscious life, despite its improbability, evolves. Alien beings decide to go on shopping trips, explorations, and visit Earth. Of course, such visits are passionately believed in by many, many people, most of whom live in California! What in your view is the likelihood of successful space travel.

**Paul:**

Suppose we do live in a universe in which not only life is inevitable, but conscious, intelligent life, too. Suppose

## ARE WE ALONE IN THE UNIVERSE?

furthermore that some fraction of intelligent life develops into technological communities. You might then conclude that the Earth should have been visited, and might still be visited today, by alien creatures. It is an argument, incidentally, often used in support of the contrary belief, that life is unique to Earth — the 'where-are-they?' argument. If the universe was teeming with life we ought to see evidence of these alien beings, and as we don't, therefore we must be alone. My feeling about this is that if life does develop to the point of technology, it makes no sense at all to travel in the flesh from one star system to another. It is immensely expensive. It is one thing to travel from planet to planet within a given star system — we will be able to do that soon — but travelling between star systems is quite another thing. The distances are so immense: the *nearest* star is $4\frac{1}{3}$ light years away from Earth.

**Phillip:**
Turn it into kilometres or miles.

**Paul:**
A light year is about ten trillion kilometres or six trillion miles. To put that into comparison, light takes a second or so to reach Earth from the moon, and about $8\frac{1}{2}$ minutes to reach us from the sun, which is a 150 million kilometres away. We're talking $4\frac{1}{3}$ *years* to the nearest star. Now if the

universe is teeming with life, as some people suggest, and if there are many, many technological communities out there, physical space travel would be a poor way to make contact. It would make much more sense for an alien civilisation to log onto the nearest node of the galactic internet and upload the video of their planet to their friendly alien neighbours next door, than to literally travel there in the flesh. The cost of interstellar travel is so horrendous that it makes no ecological or economic sense to do it. If there's an intelligent community out there that can communicate, we could contact them much, much less expensively by radio or laser once we know where they are located.

**Phillip:**

Then, of course, there is the problem of the timing. Our planet has existed for four billion years, while something approaching the human being has been around for a mere four million years. And that human being has been capable of sending radio signals for only about four decades. So you would need some amazing synchronicities to be occurring.

**Paul:**

That's absolutely right. A lot of people have an image of alien beings that are only a few decades ahead of us technologically. They don't realise how improbable this is. As you point out, life on Earth has taken about four billion

## ARE WE ALONE IN THE UNIVERSE?

years to evolve to the point of technological society. Now supposing, hypothetically, there was another planet out there where life got going at exactly the same time as it did here on Earth. There have been so many accidents of evolution, so many little byways in the evolutionary process, that the chances of the same sequence happening on another planet, reaching the same point of development to within 100 years or so of us is infinitesimal. That is why I don't believe the UFO stories because the reported aliens are just too much like us, not only in bodily form, but in their level of technology. If you read the reports, UFOs seem to be something like the next generation of stealth bombers! Just 100 or 200 years ahead of us technologically. The chances that any two planets would arrive at that similar level of technology after four billion years of evolution are simply infinitesimal. Then take into account the fact that there have been stars around for billions of years before our solar system even formed. There could be planets — and indeed life forms — that stretch back for many more billions of years than life on Earth. The conclusion you arrive at is if there are other intelligent beings out there, they will either be way, way ahead of us technologically, or way, way behind. If the latter is the case, they won't be signalling us across interstellar space. So if we do succeed at SETI and pick up an alien signal, it is likely to be from a civilisation enormously more advanced than ours.

## More Big Questions

**Phillip:**

Previously, I quoted Asimov's term 'the armies of the night', which he used to describe the serried ranks of those opposed to science. You might also argue that the term could be applied to believers in the UFO phenomenon, although in this case the armies of the night are people with a passionate love of science. They love science to such excess it would seem that they have turned the UFO into a sort of twentieth-century religion. There is a paradox here.

**Paul:**

I think that the UFO scene really *is* religion with a thin veneer of science. What is happening is that old fairy stories or Bible stories of religious visitation have been overlaid with technological language. I was always impressed by Ezekiel's vision of four flying wheels, full of eyes, out of which stepped an angel with the likeness of a man. Replace 'wheel' by disc, 'eyes' by portholes, and 'angel' by Ufonaut, and you have a classic flying saucer story!

**Phillip:**

America's energetic pop culture has given us a series of fads. There's been the yo-yo, the frisbee, the hula hoop and the flying saucer — all things, I point out, that spin. Now the latest phenomenon is, of course, the bodily abduction, as big a fad as the yo-yo. I was recently alarmed when I met

## ARE WE ALONE IN THE UNIVERSE?

and talked with a professor from Harvard who's a passionate believer in bodily abductions, having interviewed, he says, simply hundreds of abductees. Your view on this please.

**Paul:**

I have my own theory about alien abductions. It may not explain all of the cases, but I think it explains some. The abduction stories have many features in common with a phenomenon known as lucid dreaming. I'm not talking about vivid dreams; we all have vivid dreams. There's another type of dream state, quite different, which most people will have spontaneously perhaps only once or twice in their lifetime. I have certainly had lucid dreams. How do they differ from ordinary ones? In a normal dream everything has a sort of wishy-washy quality. By contrast, in a lucid dream things take on a type of reality which is every bit as sharp and real as you and me sitting here now. If you are not aware that you are having a lucid dream — these days I always am, but if you didn't know it — it could be quite terrifying. A well-known feature of the normal dream state is a sense of paralysis. We've all had that dream where we are trying unsuccessfully to run away from things. If you get that feeling in a lucid dream it can be really very scary — I have had the experience myself. Another prominent dream image is levitation, a sense of floating or flying. Again, it can occur in the lucid dream state, too. There can also be a strong

MORE BIG QUESTIONS

sense of a malevolent presence. When I have a lucid dream, I usually think that somebody has broken into the house, and they are in the room, standing at the end of the bed.

Phillip:

So you are suggesting that these dreams can be conflated with reality?

Paul:

Well, you see, if you put all those elements together you have many of the aspects of alien abduction. Somebody falls asleep, in the middle of the night they have a sense of a malevolent presence nearby, they are paralysed, and find themselves floating. The other distinctive feature of lucid dreams is that you have a strong sense of touch. Again, in the lucid dreams I've had, it is usually a feeling of something prodding or poking me. When I was a child and would have these dreams, I thought the cat was walking over me.

Phillip:

Okay, I can accept that, particularly if the dreams are then to some extent choreographed by a mass media or given a form and structure. Now I would be remiss if I didn't ask you a final question, and that is the wormhole argument. The late astronomer Carl Sagan suggested that it may be

## ARE WE ALONE IN THE UNIVERSE?

possible for interplanetary, intergalactic, cosmic visitations to occur through the wormhole. Your response?

**Paul:**

It is quite interesting, historically, what happened here. Carl Sagan wrote the book *Contact*, now a movie starring Jodie Foster. It features a so-called wormhole as an imaginary mode of faster-than-light space travel. When Sagan finished the book he went to his friend Kip Thorne at Caltech to discover if rapid transit through a wormhole could really be done. So there began a sort of recreational mathematical exercise to see if it was possible to have a shortcut between two points in space that would enable rapid transportation from one place to the other. It is already known that black holes can do funny things to space and time, and Sagan's hypothetical wormhole is somewhat like an adaptation of a black hole. As a result of these theoretical studies, Thorne and his colleagues decided that it was just about feasible — not a very practical proposition — but just about feasible that you could have such a wormhole. But there was a bizarre twist to this conclusion. It turned out that if you could go through the wormhole and come out the other end a short time later, maybe only a few minutes later, then the wormhole could also be used as a time machine, it could send you back in time! So most of the theoretical work that has since been done involves looking at mathematical models of wormholes in the context of time travel rather than space travel. However, it does look like it is theoretically possible to create a wormhole and use it for space travel, but it would certainly be a very expensive exercise.

## SELECTED READING

Paul Davies, *Are We Alone?*, Penguin, London and Melbourne, 1995.

Paul Davies, *The Fifth Miracle*, Viking, Melbourne, 1998.

Steven Dick, *The Biological Universe*, Cambridge University Press, Cambridge, 1996.

Francis Drake and Dava Sobel, *Is Anyone Out There?*, Delacorte Press, New York, 1992.

Michael Lemonick, *Other Worlds*, Simon & Schuster, New York, 1998.

Carl Sagan, *Communication With Extraterrestrial Intelligence*, MIT Press, Cambridge, Mass., 1973.

Walter Sullivan, *We Are Not Alone*, McGraw-Hill, New York, 1964.

FOUR

# DOES GOD PLAY DICE?

**Phillip:**

Of all the weird and wonderful ideas to come out of science, perhaps the most weird and the most wonderful is quantum mechanics. The great Danish physicist Niels Bohr once said that anybody who isn't shocked by quantum mechanics hasn't understood it. Well, I'm certainly shocked by it, not to say completely nonplussed, even though I have only just glimpsed the surface of this bizarre subject.

Let's admit that the word 'quantum' doesn't make sense to most people and they get it utterly wrong. When people talk of a 'quantum leap' they imagine it to be something big. But the opposite is true.

**Paul:**

The word quantum literally means 'package' or 'discrete packet' in Latin, and it was first coined by the German theoretical physicist Max Plank in 1900. Planck discovered that electromagnetic radiation like heat and light doesn't come in continuous amounts of energy, but in little packets, or quanta. Those particular quanta we now call photons.

**MORE BIG QUESTIONS**

Phillip:

So a quantum leap is in fact what?

Paul:

A quantum leap in the case of heat radiation or light is a very tiny discontinuous jump in energy, for example when a photon of light is emitted or absorbed by an atom.

Phillip:

I have hinted at quantum weirdness. Perhaps you might be kind enough to give us some examples?

Paul:

In daily life we are very familiar with notions of cause and effect, of things behaving in an orderly and predictable manner. When you get down to the microscopic realm of atoms and molecules, however, some pretty peculiar things happen, things that not only defy commonsense but look to be just plain impossible. A couple of examples of this may help. Imagine a small ordinary ball is an atom, or better still, an electron. It would do all sorts of things that we would normally regard as miraculous. Suppose I were to throw the ball at a window, one of two things will happen. As a ball it is either going to bounce back or it is going to break the window and go through. But if it was an electron, it would be possible for it to do something else entirely: it could pass through the window and come out the other side without breaking the glass! In other words it could, as we say, 'tunnel' through the barrier and appear on the other side.

To give another example: suppose I were to roll the ball along the surface of a table. Of course it will drop off the edge. Again, however, if it were an electron, it would be quite likely to bounce back off the edge. Imagine playing snooker, and when the snooker ball reaches the pocket, it bounces back at you! If you saw that sort of thing in daily life, you would think it was absolutely miraculous, totally impossible. But such phenomena happen all the time at the atomic level.

**Phillip:**

Paul, you are going to have to convince me that this sort of Lewis Carroll, Monty Pythonist weirdness is not simply a mind game played by the likes of you!

**Paul:**

Oh it happens all right. And it actually has practical applications. You can make quantum devices, in fact we are surrounded by them. Many of today's electronic gizmos, like the silicon chip, employ quantum principles. In fact, when I was a student there was something called a tunnel diode, which actually used the tunnelling effect I described, like the ball going through the window, as a practical device.

**Phillip:**
What did it actually do?

**Paul:**
The electrons tunnel through a little barrier inside, a bit like a transistor *(see Fig. 2)*. These days electronic devices can be fabricated at the level of individual atomic layers, and all of them make use of quantum properties to a greater or lesser extent. The fact that electrons can tunnel through barriers, appear and disappear, and in effect be in two places at once — all of these things — are put to practical use.

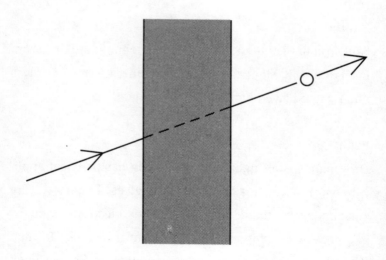

Tunnel effect. A quantum particle strikes a barrier and reappears on the far side without disrupting the barrier. In effect, it tunnels through. This is the basis of practical electronic devices.

**Phillip:**

Paul, I'm trying desperately, but I remain to be convinced. Do you have another example?

**Paul:**

Remember old-fashioned alarm clocks? They won't let you buy one any more because they are radioactive. Such clocks are luminous — coated with radium, I think — which makes them glow in the dark. And it is there that we see the tunnel effect at work, because the decay of the radium nuclei involves the emission of so-called alpha particles — the particles that Lord Rutherford famously experimented with to determine the structure of the atom. The alpha particles escape from the radium nuclei by tunnelling their way out. If they were just ordinary, common-or-garden, everyday-type particles, they wouldn't be able to get out of the nuclei. Once they have escaped, they fly off and deliver energy to the atoms around them, and that makes the clock glow. So here we see the tunnel effect actually at work. That is quantum weirdness before your very eyes!

**Phillip:**

And it's one more reason to hate an alarm clock.

**Paul:**

Oh, yes — it rings a bell too!

MORE BIG QUESTIONS

**Phillip:**

All things considered, is quantum technology much use? What are its prospects?

**Paul:**

The ultimate practical device that people are working on, but haven't yet built, is the quantum computer. This would be a computer that processes information at the quantum level, using quite different computational principles from the traditional computer, which as far as the processing operations are concerned is really a sort of clunk-clunk everyday-physics type of thing.

**Phillip:**

And the advantage of the quantum computer would be?

**Paul:**

It could compute things that no ordinary computer could achieve in a million years. Let me give you an example — actually, it's a rather famous one called the travelling salesman problem. There are twenty cities which a travelling salesman has to visit, each once and only once. The problem is to work out an itinerary that minimises the total distance travelled. It's a classic problem. If you give that to a normal computer to solve, it takes a very, very long time. And if you give it the route between forty cities to calculate, it takes much longer

## DOES GOD PLAY DICE?

than twice the time it took to solve the problem for twenty cities. However, a quantum computer could probably crack the travelling salesman problem in pretty short order, for reasons I shall come to shortly, although a rigorous proof of that is still lacking.

**Phillip:**

To move on a bit, why was Einstein a Doubting Thomas?

**Paul:**

It is very curious historically, because Einstein was actually one of the originators of the quantum theory. In 1905 he explained the photoelectric effect — the basis of the solar cell in, for example, solar panels —using Planck's idea of photons of light. But in later years he came to hate the whole theory, and by the time he died he absolutely refused to accept that quantum theory was the last word. But he was very isolated in adopting this attitude.

**Phillip:**

He thought it was inelegant in a way didn't he, or eccentric?

**Paul:**

In the early days of quantum mechanics, Einstein suspected that the theory was just plain wrong. He endeavoured to dream up imaginary experiments that would expose some sort of logical inconsistency. In the event, his opponents always wore him down by forceful argument, and eventually he conceded that there was nothing actually contradictory about the theory, in spite of its bizarre effects. So he retreated to a position where he said that quantum theory is right as far as it goes, but it is fundamentally *incomplete*. There must be some other processes going on, he insisted, that we simply don't see — perhaps on some smaller scale of size or something — a deeper level of reality.

What really bugged Einstein about quantum mechanics is the uncertainty that is involved. Let me explain. There is something called Heisenberg's uncertainty principle. Werner Heisenberg was one of the originators of the theory, and his principle says, basically, that there is a limit to what we can know about what is going on at the atomic level. I'll give you an example. There is a famous symbol, isn't there, for the atom. It's a nucleus with three orbits around it *(see Fig. 3)*. Everyone recognises that symbol as an atom. Most people

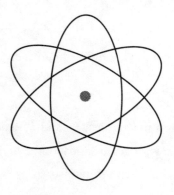

The international symbol for the atom, depicting three well-defined electron orbits around a nucleus.

assume that it is a picture of an atom which is not too far 'from the truth. An atom has a nucleus in the middle and the electrons go around it, rather like the planets go around the sun. So if one asks the question at any given time: 'Where is the electron and how is it moving?', they imagine that there must be a well-defined answer, even if we don't have the equipment to actually see.

Most people generally suppose that the electron must always *be* somewhere and must always be moving in a certain way. Well, the uncertainty principle states that this isn't so. It is simply not possible to say at any given instant *both* where the electron is and how it is moving. You can have the one or the other. You can look very carefully and you can see an electron located at a place, but then its speed is completely indeterminate. Alternatively you can measure the electron having a speed, but then its position is indeterminate. So there is a trade off.

**Phillip:**
This is a very exasperating notion and I'm not surprised Einstein was irritable.

**Paul:**
It certainly makes reality seem very slippery at the atomic level — it means that you can never pin anything down. There is a fuzziness on the atomic and subatomic scales of

size. The electron has only a form of half-existence. If you seek its location, what you get is an entity that we might call 'an electron-at-a-place'. Likewise, if you seek its motion you get 'an electron-with-a-speed'. But an electron can never have a full set of physical attributes (that is, a place and a speed) at once, as we imagine a billiard ball has.

**Phillip:**

Paul, was this anxiety, this irritation, this sense of incompleteness, what provoked Einstein into uttering probably his most famous single statement: 'God doesn't play dice with the universe'.

**Paul:**

That's right. You see, if you are uncertain about where an electron is and how it is moving, and if that uncertainty has nothing to do with your technological limitations — in other words it is intrinsic to nature, that the electron really is uncertain *in itself* as to where it is and how it is moving — then it means you can't predict from moment to moment what is going to happen. In daily life we have the notion that if you throw a ball in the air, you can accurately predict where it is going to land, and if you throw it again in the same way it will land in much the same place. In other words nature is repeatable and dependable. But at the atomic level this is no longer so. You can set up identical

### DOES GOD PLAY DICE?

systems in identical states and they will do different things. For example, you can fire an electron at a target and it bounces to the left, then you repeat the experiment with *identical* circumstances and it will bounce to the right! And all you can do is give the betting odds — you can say 50–50, or 40–60 — to the left or the right.

The rules of quantum mechanics forbid you from saying in any individual case what will happen. So quantum theory is basically a statistical theory, like roulette or dice. You can only give the odds. Although quite precise and mathematical from the statistical point of view, you generally cannot say in any particular case what the outcome is going to be. Einstein hated that idea. He hated the notion that the future was intrinsically indeterminate.

**Phillip:**

What is the situation with the left-or-right scattering experiment if, in a moment of sloth, you don't look and see which way it bounced in any particular case?

**Paul:**

What you have to conclude in that case, according to the rules of quantum physics, is that there are two possible worlds: one with a left-moving electron, the other with a right-moving electron, and both of these worlds somehow co-exist in a hybrid reality.

## MORE BIG QUESTIONS

**Phillip:**

When you say something like that, as simply and as matter-of-factly as you do, to what extent do you really, deeply comprehend and know it?

**Paul:**

Oh, I think I understand what is happening. At least, it is not a problem for me to imagine two worlds with two different things going on, projected on top of each other to form a hybrid, or overlapping reality. It is like taking two movies and projecting them onto the same screen although this simplifies things a bit because a quantum superposition entails an *interference* of images, not just an overlap.

**Phillip:**

Is it limited to two?

**Paul:**

No, it's not.

**Phillip:**

Does the theory not allow for an infinity of possibilities?

**Paul:**

Absolutely right, it does indeed. In the more general situation there are infinite possible outcomes of a scattering event or some other atomic process, and we must imagine an infinite number of alternative realities — or contenders for reality — superimposed upon each other; a superimposed reality. In this amalgam of possible worlds, each individual contender is a sort of ghostly half-reality — it is less than real, in the sense that true reality comes only when we look and see what is actually happening. Only when an observation is made can we be sure as to which of these outcomes has actually taken place. So I would refer to these contending realities, these alternative universes, as merely potential worlds, not actually existing worlds.

**Phillip:**
So each is not as good as the other, they don't have the same status?

**Paul:**
No, each has the same status. But it is only when you actually make an observation (or at least, when some observation-like physical process takes place) that you concretise one of those abstract or ghostly possibilities.

Now I have to say right here that many of my colleagues profoundly disagree with that. They believe that these alternative worlds are equally real, and that they exist as parallel universes. So if you fire an electron at a target and it may go to the left or it may go to the right, the universe

MORE BIG QUESTIONS

effectively splits into two, one universe with a left moving-electron and one with a right-moving electron. (Alternatively, two identical parallel copies of the universe differentiate at that point.)

Phillip:

Given that there are an infinite number of observations one could make, this means that there are infinite infinities of alternatives, options.

Paul:

Exactly. We might call it a 'multiverse', or an infinite number of parallel universes, or parallel realities. This way of looking at quantum mechanics is called the 'many-worlds interpretation'. It is very popular. Incidentally, it also helps one to understand why a quantum computer would be so powerful. In effect it would be able to compute in all these parallel worlds at once, and combine the results to get the output.

Phillip:

When I get disturbed, emotionally rattled, I sometimes feel the need for a pet, they're very soothing. So we might introduce at this stage Schrödinger's pussy.

Phillip:

Yes! Cat lovers, please skip the next couple of pages! Erwin

DOES GOD PLAY DICE?

Schrödinger, one of the founders of quantum physics in the 1920s, devised a famous thought experiment involving a cat (it has never been done in practice). Its purpose was to demonstrate on an everyday scale of size the bizarre nature of atomic processes. I guess most people can accept that atoms are strange little things, but as you don't run into them individually in daily life, it doesn't really seem to matter if something weird is going on at the atomic scale. However, if something funny happened on an everyday scale of size — if we saw two contending realities in a room for example — we would find that very shocking.

Schrödinger's cat experiment aims to produce just such a state of affairs. What happens is this. The pussycat is put in a box along with a flask of cyanide and a hammer, and a triggering device that will cause the hammer to smash the flask if set off by an atomic process like the decay of a radioactive nucleus. Now if you apply the rules of quantum mechanics to the entire contents of the box, including the cat (which is, after all, made of atoms), then what you are to suppose is as follows. After running the experiment for, say, one minute, there is a 50–50 chance that the atom will decay, trigger the hammer, break the flask and kill the cat. According to the rules of quantum mechanics, if you don't look and see, if you don't actually open the box and check if the cat is alive or dead, you are forced to conclude that the cat is in a superposition of live and dead states. In other

MORE BIG QUESTIONS

words, it is in a hybrid state of 'part-aliveness' and 'part-deadness', whatever that means. The experiment is really a *reductio ad absurdum* argument, because presumably the cat knows whether it is alive or dead! However, it starkly illustrates the need to address the whole issue about what it takes to prompt or provoke nature into making up its mind about which of the contending realities it wants. Does it take a person peering in a box to effect this concretisation, or does it take a cat, or could a computer or a camera or some simpler device prompt, as it were, 'nature' into making up its mind? Well, there is no agreed answer to this.

**Phillip:**

But in what you are describing, nature doesn't need to make up its mind. Nature simply allows for every possibility.

**Paul:**

That's right, but the question is, are all these possibilities *really* there? Are they co-existing in parallel? Or is there only one reality, one universe, and if so, how does it get selected from the myriad realities on offer?

**Phillip:**

Parallel universes — a mind-boggling notion. Are you suggesting that there are universes in which Tony Blair lost the last British general election?

### Paul:

That's right, yes. According to the theory — if you subscribe to this particular many-universes interpretation (which many of my senior colleagues do, I might say) — these contending realities are *really there*. In other words, quantum physics tells us that there isn't one universe — there is an infinity of them. All of the different possibilities, all of the things that are possible at the atomic level and above, are really happening somewhere. Not over here or over there in our space and time, but in some parallel reality.

### Phillip:

Are there Luddites who take an alternative view to this, who are hostile to this interpretation of quantum mechanics?

### Paul:

Yes, there are. I would say that during my career there's been a decisive shift towards the many-universes view of interpreting quantum mechanics. Possibly a majority of the senior figures working in this area of theoretical physics now would regard themselves as backing the many-universes theory, but there are certainly four or five other ways of interpreting what is going on.

I can tell you what the party line is. Niels Bohr, who was a bit like the father figure in the early days of quantum theory, pointed out that we have the commonsense world

MORE BIG QUESTIONS

of everyday experience, often called the world of classical physics, and then there is this madhouse quantum world down at the micro-level. Somehow we have to interface the two. But where is that interface? Bohr realised that at some point the peculiar quantum world would have to go over into the everyday commonsense world of classical physics, but he was very coy about where that transition took place, and how it could be that one sort of physics would turn into another sort.

Today, I think that most of my colleagues would take the view that if quantum physics is the correct theory of the universe, then it has to apply to everything, even to the everyday world. The fact that we don't notice peculiar effects occurring on an everyday scale is because something within quantum mechanics brings about the transition to an apparently classical reality. But there is no agreement on what that thing is.

**Phillip:**
I'm very grateful that we don't notice bizarre quantum effects in daily life, Paul.

**Paul:**
Well, we don't. Except, I should point out, that it is not physical size as such that counts. For example, superconductivity (the flow of electricity without any resistance

DOES GOD PLAY DICE?

that occurs in some materials at low temperatures) is a quantum phenomenon, but a superconductor can be, say, centimetres in size. Whatever it is that makes the properties of the quantum world approach those of the normal classical world, is going to be something more complicated than size. It could be, for example, the complexity of the system or its gravitational arrangement. It seems to have something to do with the number and nature of participating components. But we don't know. We don't know what it is that causes the quantum world to turn into the classical world.

**Phillip:**

Are you saying that there are two parallel sets of laws operating in nature, one for the quantum micro-world and the other for the everyday classical world?

**Paul:**

Oh no! There is only one set of laws for the whole universe. Physicists believe the quantum laws are the more fundamental, and that in principle they apply to everything, including everyday objects like tables and chairs. It's just that distinctively quantum effects would be exceedingly small on a macroscopic scale, so we don't notice them. The challenge is to understand by what physical process an apparently classical world emerges from its underlying

## MORE BIG QUESTIONS

quantum nature. In other words, we would like to derive the laws of classical mechanics as approximations of the deeper laws of quantum mechanics, and on the way answer the question about what it takes for a system to behave in an approximately classical manner.

My own feeling is that these potential realities I have been discussing are not *really* real. Instead what happens is that when the quantum system that we are considering becomes sufficiently complex (and I think a cat is complex enough), then it makes the transition to the familiar everyday commonsense world.

**Phillip:**

Like a form of a gravitational pull that destroys the quantum properties.

**Paul:**

I'm not sure it is literally gravitational, although Oxford mathematician Roger Penrose has suggested it might be. Personally, I think it is the complexity of the system. I believe that if the system is complex enough, then the rules of the game change. However, I'm in a minority of about two in taking that point of view!

**Phillip:**

But I've got a terrible feeling that another interview is being conducted in an identical room where you're taking a completely different position.

**Paul:**

Yes, that is exactly right according to the many-universes view. Not only are there all these different realities, but many of them are inhabited by beings who are almost carbon copies of ourselves. So there will indeed be another universe somewhere with a Paul Davies and Phillip Adams having a slightly different — even infinitesimally different — conversation!

**Phillip:**

This raises the issue of the way the human mind is entangled in the ultimate reality of the cosmos, because you are now dealing with our perceptions of it.

**Paul:**

Indeed. That's actually the whole point. The really disturbing thing about quantum physics is that it does seem in some way to involve the observer. It entangles the observer and the observed in a very intimate way. You see, in the old-fashioned classical physics, the observer was just there for the ride. In Newton's scheme, for example, there certainly could be observers, but they didn't really matter very much. Now it has to be conceded that in any physical theory

## MORE BIG QUESTIONS

observers disturb the system they are observing. Suppose you want to measure the temperature of, say, a glass of water. You put a thermometer into the water; the very act of doing this will change the temperature of the water you are trying to measure. Never mind, you can compensate for that. In principle, you can take the disturbance completely into account and, by compensating for it, you can make the measurement as accurately as you like.

But when it comes to quantum physics the situation is dramatically different. The act of measurement will disturb the system that you are trying to measure in a way that can *never* be taken into account with any certainty. In other words, quantum phenomena enfold or entangle the observer with the observed in a manner that simply can't be untangled. This entanglement seems to bring something like 'mind', something like 'observer', into nature in a very intimate way. Now that is anathema to most scientists, who struggle to keep mind and subjectivity out. The retreat into the many-universes interpretation is really one way of trying to evade introducing the observer at all, because you don't have to say that a cat is good enough or a human being is good enough to effect the actualisation of reality, or that something strange and mystical happens when an observation is made. You simply declare that all the possible quantum alternatives are acted out in their own universes in their own way. They are all parallel realities, and everything that

DOES GOD PLAY DICE?

can happen, does happen. So it neatly evades having to introduce the observer in a crucial way.

My feeling about circumventing the observation problem by introducing many universes is that it is a big missed opportunity. Any complete theory of the universe — and quantum mechanics claims to be such a theory — has to explain observers. It has to tell us why there are such things as observers and observations. So it seems to me this is the one place we should be actually looking to explain the existence of observation and mind and so on. To try to define it away by having all these parallel worlds seems to me like a missed opportunity.

**Phillip:**

Could it be possible that at the moment of the singularity, at the moment of the big bang, there were alternative universes created, universes in which the mathematics didn't work out?

**Paul:**

So far, all that I have been discussing assumes that the mathematics is the same; that is, there are fixed underlying quantum laws, and all that is happening is that different alternatives which are available within the scope of those fixed laws are acted out. However, one can certainly extend the general concept, and consider alternative parallel

MORE BIG QUESTIONS

universes in which the underlying laws and forces and so on have a different mathematical form. In most of these universes the laws of physics would not permit life and they would go unobserved.

Of course, this whole topic comes into it's own in the subject of cosmology, the study of the universe as a whole. In the field known as quantum cosmology, we apply quantum physics to the entire universe as an integral system. Now you might object and say 'Well, hang on a minute. Quantum physics is about little things like atoms, while cosmology is about the universe, which is pretty big. How can you apply quantum theory to the universe?' The answer is that the universe is expanding, so it must once have been very shrunken. Just after the big bang that started the universe off, all matter was compressed to atomic dimensions, and quantum physics must at that time have made a significant difference. We believe that the universe was born as a quantum event, and somehow, at an early stage (in the first tiny fraction of a second), it made the transition from fuzzy quasi-reality to the concrete reality of the cosmos we observe today. Space and time, large material objects with well-defined properties, definite forces of nature — these things somehow emerged from the ghostly maelstrom of the quantum origin.

The question is how to interpret the rules of quantum mechanics when applied to the entire cosmos. If you are

DOES GOD PLAY DICE?

one of those people who believes that the observer matters, then you have a problem with quantum cosmology, because if you apply quantum physics to the whole universe you can't get outside the universe to observe it. The universe is everything that there is. There are no external observers, by definition. The many-universes people are okay on this point because they can just assume that all possible universes that can exist get created, and then act out their alternative histories in parallel. So, for example, just as we see a universe like ours which is expanding from some initial singularity to an uncertain future, well there would be another universe which has not expanded so far as ours and would already be collapsing. There would be yet another that would be expanding much faster, and would already be nearly devoid of matter because the galaxies would have flown very far apart. All of these universes are there together.

**Phillip:**

To try to contain these notions within your neurones and synapses must be a bit of a strain. How do quantum mechanics stay sane?

**Paul:**

The one thing I would recommend is: don't try to visualise it. There is a perception, I think, among the public that if something can't be visualised — if you can't see it in your

MORE BIG QUESTIONS

mind's eye — then it can't be so. People write to me in quite exasperated tones and assert that this or that physical theory can't be true because it makes no sense to them. 'I can't imagine it', they complain.

But what is commonsense after all? Something that has been honed by evolution. Darwinian evolution has equipped us to survive in the jungle, not to do atomic physics or cosmology. As a result, we are quite good at jumping across rivers, catching falling apples, and doing all sorts of everyday things that have to do with avoiding predators and obtaining food. There is no reason at all why Darwinian evolution should equip us for understanding what is going on inside atoms because they are simply not relevant to surviving in the jungle.

The same thing applies to black holes and curved space and all the other weird phenomena out there in the cosmos. We find them hard to understand because there is no good evolutionary reason why we should understand them at a commonsense or intuitive level. That is the power of science. The great thing about science is that it can take us into territory where commonsense and everyday intuition are left behind.

Phillip:
Are you suggesting that science can take us beyond the reach of evolution?

**Paul:**

It takes us beyond the reach of commonsense. Evolution has equipped us for commonsense and for visualisation, if you like, of everyday states of affairs, strategies that have survival value. There is no survival value in being able to visualise what is going on inside an atom, and yet we can still come to understand atoms in a certain way without this inner visualisation or intuition! We achieve this by using mathematics as our sure guide. So: 'Abandon commonsense all ye who enter here.' If you remain wedded to commonsense ideas of reality when you tackle topics like quantum mechanics, you can be sure that they will lead you astray.

## SELECTED READING

David Albert, *Quantum Mechanics and Experience*, Harvard University Press, Harvard, Mass., 1992.

Paul Davies, *Other Worlds*, Penguin, London and Melbourne, 1990.

Paul Davies and Julian Brown, *The Ghost in the Atom*, Cambridge University Press, Cambridge, 1986.

David Deutsch, *The Fabric of Reality*, Viking, London 1997.

John Gribbin, *In Search of Schrödinger's Cat*, Wildwood House, London, 1984.

Alastair Rae, *Quantum Physics: Illusion or Reality?*, Cambridge University Press, Cambridge, 1986.

Euan Squires, *The Mystery of the Quantum World* (second edition), IOP Publishing, Bristol, 1994.

F I V E

# EINSTEIN'S LEGACY

**Phillip:**

Einstein's theory of relativity is an icon for the baffling side of twentieth-century science. It is abstract, mathematical, and notoriously difficult to grasp. It has given us such mind-numbing oddities as timewarps and curved space, black holes, big bangs and singularities, to name but a few. Yet this theory is now an established part of mainstream physics, taught to every undergraduate. It has even given us practical applications. So what is all the fuss about?

**Paul:**

The special theory of relativity, which was published by Albert Einstein in 1905, is a theory of space, time and motion. Prior to this theory, everybody regarded space and time as absolute and universal; if you like, they were simply *there*. Then Einstein demonstrated that space and time are, in fact, relative; things such as the length of objects and the duration between events depend on how the observer is moving. One consequence is that space and time are not independent of each other, but instead form a single four-dimensional 'continuum' known as spacetime. In a nutshell, the theory says that if you move close to the speed of light, strange things happen to space and time — they become 'warped'. One consequence is that the speed of light is a barrier in this theory. It's the fastest speed that an object can move.

**Phillip:**
I find that immensely frustrating. Please tell me why I may not go faster.

**Paul:**
Suppose you try and do it. Suppose you try to make something travel faster than light by simply continually accelerating it. Physicists routinely do this in the laboratory. They have giant accelerator machines that whirl subatomic particles around them at very high speeds. Now if you keep pushing and pushing, what happens is that instead of the particles going faster and faster, they just get heavier and heavier. This is one of the manifestations of the famous formula $E = mc^2$, which tells us that mass (m) is a form of energy (E). The factor c stands for the speed of light and is a very big number, which means that a little bit of mass is worth an awful lot of energy. The formula also implies that energy has mass, and thus weight. For example, a hot saucepan weighs a tiny bit more than a cold saucepan.

## MORE BIG QUESTIONS

Also, a box full of light is a fraction heavier than an empty box.

Well, motion is a form of energy, too, so a moving particle will be heavier than a stationary one. If you try to make the particle go faster, less and less of the added energy appears as extra speed, and more and more goes into making additional mass. As the speed of light is approached, the energy is almost all in the mass. Getting more speed becomes a matter of diminishing returns. So the speed of light acts like a barrier. The particles just get heavier and heavier, you can't push them on through that limiting speed. People often ask, 'Why not? Why can't you break the light barrier?' The answer is that it is a law of nature. I don't know what else to say, that's just the way nature is. It is structured in such a way that the speed of light is an absolute barrier to motion.

**Phillip:**

I had no idea that the special theory was such a doddle. What about the general theory that was added about ten years later?

**Paul:**

The general theory was published in late 1915. Einstein struggled to put it together over a number of years. It was very much a personal effort, whereas the special theory was the amalgamation of a number of contributions. The

EINSTEIN'S LEGACY

general theory of relativity is also a theory of space, time and motion, but it includes the effects of gravitation. Einstein had the brilliant insight that gravitation isn't really a force, as Newton had proposed — the force of gravity. Einstein said no, it is not a force at all, it is really a warping or distortion of the geometry of space and time. Technically, we say that 'spacetime is curved'. That sounds very mysterious, doesn't it? But it is actually quite an easy idea. At school we learn the rules of geometry on flat sheets of paper — for example, that the angles of a flat triangle add up to 180 degrees — and we normally think of three-dimensional space as obeying the same 'flat' geometrical rules. It turns out, however, that gravitational fields have the effect of changing those rules by introducing a sort of curvature or distortion in this geometry. For example, the angles of a big triangle drawn in the three-dimensional space around the sun would not add up to 180 degrees because the sun's gravitational field slightly alters the geometry in its vicinity (see Fig. 4). The effect is only very small for the sun, although it can be detected by mapping the positions of the astronomical bodies very accurately, which, in practice, is best done by bouncing radar signals off the planets. Crudely speaking, the stronger the gravitational field the more that space (strictly speaking, spacetime) is bent or curved. So the general theory of relativity ties together gravitation, space, time and motion into a unified mathematical description.

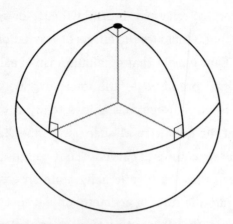

On the surface of a sphere, a triangle may contain three right angles, adding to 270°.

**Phillip:**

Paul, so much for the theory, but are there any technological whistles and bells, any gizmos that you could tell us about which exploit the theory?

**Paul:**

When Einstein first published the general theory, he predicted a number of rather tiny effects in the solar system. For example, it was already known that the orbit of Mercury slowly shifts over the centuries by small but conspicuous amounts — it is still, however, a very tiny effect. Einstein's theory explained this effect precisely; it was a great triumph. Einstein also correctly predicted that a starbeam passing close to the sun should be very slightly curved. If you look

EINSTEIN'S LEGACY

at the position of a star in the sky when the sun is in one place, it is slightly different from when the sun is in another place. It is almost like looking at the sky through a weak lens. During a solar eclipse, stars can be observed close to the sun, where the effect is greatest. It is still a very tiny effect, but it can just be measured, and the measurements confirm the theory. So there were these small effects, but they didn't seem to be any big deal, and for a long time people thought that the general theory of relativity was really quite interesting by predicting these tiny effects, but had no practical value.

Today, however, with our modern instrumentation and electronics, even these tiny effects become important. A classic example is the global positioning system that owners of yachts and even small boats use to find out where they are on the Earth's surface to a precision of within a few metres. Now this system has to take into account the effects of general relativity. If it didn't, I'm told that you could be out by up to 25 kilometres in your positioning. So here is a measurable and noticeable effect of the general theory of relativity with real practical value.

**Phillip:**
You have mentioned that Newton was wrong with his theory of gravity. But wasn't Newton's theory nonetheless a magnificent approximation?

## MORE BIG QUESTIONS

Paul:

There is no doubt about it that Newton's theory of gravitation is good for almost all purposes. It is good enough to send a spacecraft to the moon, for example. It is only when the gravitational fields become very strong, or when you need super precision, such as with aircraft navigation or your yacht on the ocean, that the general theory comes into it's own. A lot of people say, `Well, what was wrong with Newton's theory? Can't we just go with that? Why did it have to be changed? Why did Einstein have to unpick that?'

It turns out that there is a very good reason why Einstein could not accept Newton's theory of gravitation. It has to do with the speed of light again. Let me give an illustration. Newton would have said that the Earth moves around the sun in a curved path because of the sun's gravitational pull. Imagine if by magic we could make the sun go away, vanish, just like that. What would happen next? Of course the Earth would no longer be bound in its orbit and it would wander off through the galaxy. However, it takes $8\frac{1}{2}$ minutes for light to reach us from the sun, so if the sun vanished now we wouldn't see it disappear for another $8\frac{1}{2}$ minutes. But according to Newton's theory, the Earth's orbit ought to change instantly. The moment the sun ceased to exist, the Earth should fly off towards interstellar space. The reason is that in Newton's theory gravitational effects propagate instantaneously. But we have already discussed

EINSTEIN'S LEGACY

that nothing should travel faster than the speed of light, and that includes all forces and physical influences. So Einstein was obliged to adapt Newton's theory.

Newton's theory works well when the gravitational fields are weak, or the bodies involved are moving slowly compared to the speed of light, but as soon as the fields get strong and the speeds large, space and time bending effects start to manifest themselves. I suppose that the black hole is the classic example of where intense gravitational fields produce really peculiar effects.

**Phillip:**
What is a black hole?

**Paul:**
The name says it all. It is a region of space and time that is both black and empty. Now how do you form such a thing? One way is when a star runs out of fuel and collapses under it's own weight; no force in the universe can then prevent it from shrinking to effectively zero size. The force of gravity becomes so strong that it overwhelms all other forces — it will even trap light. As we have discussed, nothing can travel faster than light, so the intense gravitation sucks in and traps everything else as well, including the material of the original star. All the matter is compressed into a single point of infinite density, leaving the surrounding space

MORE BIG QUESTIONS

empty. So we are dealing with a region of space that is devoid of matter and appears black from the outside because light can't escape — hence 'black hole'. The point of infinite density is called a singularity. Strictly, it is not a physical entity, but a *boundary* of spacetime. It marks the breakdown of the theory of relativity.

**Phillip:**

Let us imagine that we are meandering in the vicinity of a black hole and we get sucked into it. What do you hypothesise happens?

**Paul:**

Nobody really knows what happens if you fall into a black hole, but we can be pretty sure that you can't get out again! You can't get out for the same reason that we have been discussing, because you can't travel faster than light, and if light itself is trapped, then you are trapped. If you take the mathematical theory as your guide, then at the centre of the black hole lies the singularity, the point where the entire matter of the original star is compressed into a single point of infinite density. In the *simplest* case — an exactly spherical black hole — it seems that you would be inexorably drawn to the singularity. In fact, it would all happen rather rapidly; in the case of a black hole with a mass equal to that of the sun, you would reach the singularity in much less

120

EINSTEIN'S LEGACY

than a millisecond (in your frame of reference) after you had entered the hole. You would hit the singularity and be completely obliterated. So it looks as if falling into a black hole is a one way journey to nowhere. However, we can't be completely sure of that because it is entirely likely that at some stage before the singularity forms, the theory of relativity breaks down (the prediction of an infinite physical quantity has always signalled a breakdown of the theory in the past) and must be replaced by something else — we don't know what. Most physicists think that quantum mechanics will have an effect, and fuzz out the infinite curvature. But the theory is still vague.

**Phillip:**

Is there any aspect of the general theory of relativity that is yet to be tested?

**Paul:**

There is one phenomenon that people have been working on for quite some time — the existence of gravitational waves. These waves would be like ripples in spacetime itself. The theory predicts that they should travel at the speed of light and carry an immense amount of energy, although their effect on ordinary matter would be so feeble that they are almost impossible to detect. Remember that gravitation is by far the weakest of nature's forces. You

MORE BIG QUESTIONS

would need fantastically sensitive technology to pick up gravitational waves passing through the lab.

**Phillip:**
How fantastic?

**Paul:**
To give you some idea, suppose I had a chunk of metal about the size of a human being. A gravitational wave passing through it would cause the metal to wobble and vibrate. But for a typical intense burst of gravitational radiation, the movement of the metal would be much, much less than the size of a single atomic nucleus. Much less. To detect gravitational waves on a regular basis, such tiny wobbles need to be registered to a level of sensitivity equivalent to measuring the change in the distance between here and the nearest star to a precision of one human hair's width!

**Phillip:**
Is anyone working on a methodology to achieve such a fantastic sensitivity?

**Paul:**
There have been people working on it for many years, including right here in Australia. David Blair and his group at the University of Western Australia have produced resonant

EINSTEIN'S LEGACY

bar detectors. Let me explain. They take a bar of metal, in their case niobium, but any metal will do, and suspend it in a vacuum very delicately to see if it shakes and shudders unaccountably. If the frequency of a passing gravitational wave happens to match the natural vibration frequency of the bar, then a resonance is set up and the movement gets amplified. The trick is to detect these vibrations electronically. Of course, they have to isolate the bar from seismic disturbances, noise, and so on, and also to cool it to a very low temperature to reduce the bar's own thermal agitation.

A better technology, now being developed around the world as well as in Australia, involves the use of lasers. Laser light is sent off along two perpendicular tubes of equal length, which form an L-shaped system. The light is reflected by mirrors at the ends. The two reflected light beams are merged, which enables, in effect, a comparison of the respective times for the light to travel down each tube *(see Fig 5)*. If a gravitational wave passes through the system, the ripples in the geometry of space serve to stretch and shrink the tubes by a tiny amount, and this could show up as a mismatch of the travel times for the laser beams. This technique offers a more sensitive way of detecting gravitational waves, and laser detectors are being built in various countries now.

Although nobody has yet detected a gravitational wave, physicists are pretty sure that they exist, not only because

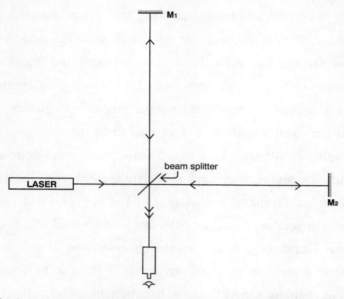

Gravitational wave detector. A laser beam is split in two, and each beamlet directed to a distant mirror, M1 and M2. The reflected beamlets are recombined and observed. If the distances to the mirrors are equal, the light waves will arrive in step and reinforce. If, however, a passing gravitational wave stretches or shrinks the distances to M1 and M2 by different amounts, the light waves may return slightly out of step. This would show up as a change in brightness.

Einstein predicted them about 80 years ago, but also because of the antics of a double-star system called a binary pulsar. It consists of two neutron stars orbiting around each other. The stars are observed to be spiralling together very slowly, and the rate of decay matches exactly Einstein's formula for the energy drain expected if gravitational waves are being given off. It's a little bit like the era before the detection of radio waves. Imagine somebody at that time giving you a radio transmitter, but you have no way of

EINSTEIN'S LEGACY

knowing if it works, if it really is emitting radio waves. You plug it in, switch on, and you notice that your electricity bills go up. The energy must be going somewhere. In the case of the binary pulsar it looks like the energy is being given off in the form of gravitational waves.

**Phillip:**

Can you imagine a consumer benefit coming out of this particular technology?

**Paul:**

I don't think it's going to be the sort of bonanza that we got from electromagnetic waves, for example radio waves, when it led to radio technology, electronics, radar and so on. However, astronomers are very keen to develop gravitational wave detectors because they are going to open up a whole new window on the universe. We currently have telescopes that use light and radio waves, gamma rays and so on; we have explored the whole of the electromagnetic spectrum. Gravitational waves represent an entirely new spectrum. Astronomers could see things with a gravitational wave telescope that you could never see with any optical or radio telescope. You could, for example, study the coalescence of two stars as they orbit together, and finally merge, maybe forming a black hole. You could peer into the heart of quasars, very energetic objects that are probably super-massive black

## MORE BIG QUESTIONS

holes eating material in their vicinity. Gravitational waves would let you observe things that you could never see in any other way. I'm sure it is going to be the trail-blazing astronomical technique of the twenty-first century.

**Phillip:**

If Einstein was currently a student in the Australian education system, I think the special theory would get him 10 out of 10 and a koala stamp, but you still are not entirely satisfied with it. What's wrong with the theory?

**Paul:**

I think the special theory is okay, but the general theory of relativity, which includes gravitation, cannot be the last word. The main problem is that the other of the twin pillars of twentieth-century physics, quantum mechanics, doesn't rest easily with the general theory of relativity. If you try to put the two theories together — if, to use the jargon, you try to quantise gravitation — then what you mostly obtain is mathematical nonsense: infinite answers to well-defined questions. Clearly there is something wrong. There have been all sorts of attempts during my career to fix up either the one theory or the other to make the merger work. At present the union is a little bit like a shotgun marriage. You take two theories, each of which is mathematically consistent on its own, and very beautiful and confirmed by experiment,

EINSTEIN'S LEGACY

and you try to amalgamate them into a theory of quantum gravity. But they don't want to be married, so you try to force them together anyhow. That is obviously unsatisfactory.

It would be much better either to change the one theory or the other, or maybe both theories. Perhaps both are some approximation to a theory at a deeper level. There are various ideas around just now. The one that is making all the running at the moment is called M-theory, which is an attempt to build up a theory of space, time and matter in terms of moving membranes. It is an elaboration of the earlier string theory, which hypothesised that perhaps the whole world is made up of little loops of string that wiggle around. So now, perhaps instead it is made out of little membranes that flap about! We just don't know. It may be something else entirely, something we haven't yet thought of. Physicists recognise that space and time, which for Newton were just an arena — they were just *there* — became, with Einstein, part of the dynamics — the laws — that govern motion, and could themselves change and move and become involved in the action. The hope and expectation is that the concepts of space and time should somehow come *out* of the theory and ought not to be put in as part of the tools of the trade.

Phillip:
Now this ambitious goal is tantalisingly close, yet elusive.

## MORE BIG QUESTIONS

### Paul:

It is a little difficult to say just how close it is. If you talk to the people working on something like M-theory, then of course they are gung-ho and reckon that the problems with the theory will be solved in pretty short order. In my opinion, to be realistic, we are a long way from having a fundamental theory that neatly integrates not only gravitation and quantum physics, but space and time as well.

### Phillip:

Is the universe still a bit like the blind man and the elephant? In other words is the nature of the universe still open for debate at this level?

### Paul:

Yes, it is still very open. There are these various bits of physical theory — I've mentioned quantum mechanics, gravitation, and the general theory of relativity. There are other areas of physics as well, for example thermodynamics, and each is pretty successful in it's own domain. The problem is to integrate them all in some way, and the biggest clash is between quantum mechanics and gravitation. That is the conundrum we really need to solve.

### Phillip:

It was a clash, of course, that Einstein felt to his dying day.

EINSTEIN'S LEGACY

**Paul:**

Einstein never believed in quantum mechanics. His hope was that his theory of gravitation — the general theory of relativity — if suitably developed, would explain all this quantum stuff. Towards the end of his life he tried very hard but unsuccessfully to formulate a grand unified theory that would include quantum effects. Or perhaps a theory that would provide a level of explanation deeper than those quantum effects, and show that at that deeper level all the weird quantum phenomena didn't happen.

**Phillip:**

Paul, I feel us being drawn back towards the black hole. Stephen Hawking made a stab at combining quantum mechanics with gravitation, didn't he? And not without some success, I believe. Would you describe Hawking's black hole evaporation effect?

**Paul:**

Hawking had the idea that, even though quantum mechanics and gravitation don't fit together in a mathematically consistent way, one can nevertheless make a start at attempting to describe a situation where both aspects of nature exercise an influence. You can apply quantum mechanics to a specific object, like a black hole, and see how you get on. It turns out that you can get some sensible

129

MORE BIG QUESTIONS

answers when you do that. What you find is that the black hole is no longer black but emits radiation, in fact a very distinctive type of radiation — heat radiation. It has the thumb print, the exact spectrum, of a body in thermodynamic equilibrium, that is, at a uniform temperature. So the black hole glows, just like an oven that has been allowed to come to a uniform temperature within.

This phenomenon raises a curious question: if the black hole is emitting heat, if it is glowing, then where is the energy coming from? $E = mc^2$ again! The energy can only come from the mass of the black hole. But the size of a black hole is determined by its mass. If a black hole loses mass, it decreases in size. If it gains mass, it grows in size. Which alternative eventuates depends on whether the hole is hotter or cooler than its environment. If the hole is hotter than the environment, it loses mass and shrinks. As a consequence of emitting heat radiation, the black hole gets smaller and smaller, that is, it evaporates. It is a very slow process, I might say. Even a black hole as small as the nucleus of an atom will take the entire lifetime of the universe to evaporate away, but eventually it will. According to the theory, it shrinks in size at an escalating rate and eventually disappears in a puff of radiation. This is the ultimate vanishing act, you have a star that implodes and forms a black hole, and thereby disappears from the universe, and then the black hole itself disappears up its own spacetime!

**Phillip:**

We introduced Carl Sagan's idea about wormholes earlier. Now that we are speculating about black holes again, just how possible is Jodie Foster's exciting ride across the galaxy?

**Paul:**

Almost possible. Earlier we were discussing what happens if you fall into a black hole. I said we don't know, and that is certainly true. The existence of wormholes is still extremely speculative; however, since a wormhole would be an adaptation of a black hole, one possibility that has been around for quite some time is that instead of hitting a singularity at the centre of a black hole, you fall right on through it and come out in another universe. A slight variation is that you might come out in a distant part of our universe. When you look at the physics of this, the wormhole might be like a tube or a tunnel connecting two different regions of spacetime, which can provide a short-cut. The gravitational fields involved would be so intense that they would tend to make the wormhole's diameter shrink. The throat of the wormhole would try to collapse and trap anything attempting to get through. The trick, if you are really seriously interested in turning this into a practical proposition, is to devise some way of keeping the throat of such a wormhole open. To do that you would need exotic types of fields that have negative energy, and all sorts of properties which have never been observed in the laboratory.

## MORE BIG QUESTIONS

**Phillip:**

No problem for you, a quantum mechanic, though.

**Paul:**

Exactly. No problem for the quantum mechanic. In fact, some of my own work has been on the negative energy that quantum field theory predicts, and the use of this negative energy to keep wormhole throats open. It's one of these sort of theoretical games that we play. I mentioned earlier that after Carl Sagan wrote *Contact*, he went to his friend Kip Thorne at Caltech and said, 'Can you and the gang check out this idea?', which they did, initially for fun. In the event, it has spawned a whole industry. There are people all around the world writing papers on wormholes, not just as devices for jumping from A to B through space in this manner, but also as time machines. So, theoretically, if you could go through a wormhole to some distant place and then come shooting back at close to the speed of light, the normal way through space, it would be possible to get back to your starting place before you left! Meaning there would be two of you!

**Phillip:**

Let's finish by looking to the future. Along comes young Einstein and wobbles the pedestal of Newton. When will another dazzling young scientist, he or she, come along and wobble Einstein's pedestal?

EINSTEIN'S LEGACY

## Paul:

I have a hunch it is going to be pretty soon. The reason I say this is that gravitation is only one of four fundamental forces of nature. The other three are electromagnetism, and two nuclear forces called weak and strong. I think most physicists believe that these four forces ought to be integrated or unified into a single superforce. Somehow we have to draw gravitation, which has this very peculiar description in terms of geometry and the warping of spacetime, in with the other three forces that have more conventional descriptions. The theory of gravitation is obviously ripe for modification. Where I would say that Einstein's work will stand the test of time is in the special theory, the no-faster-than-light rule, for example, and $E = mc^2$. Also, the weird effects that act when you get close to the speed of light — the space and time distortions. I think those ideas are here to stay.

## Phillip:

Will the next great equation be written on a single blackboard, by a single hand, and be a product of a single mind, or will it be the consequence of a collective effort?

## Paul:

This is an interesting question, isn't it, about the history of science. You look back and ask what ideas came out of the

## MORE BIG QUESTIONS

scientific culture and what was a product of individual genius. Einstein himself is supposed to be the archetypal scientific genius, beavering away on his own and producing great thoughts. As I mentioned earlier, the general theory of relativity was largely a product of his own intellect, whereas with the special theory he drew upon a number of contributions from other people.

Could anybody today command the subject of physics with the authority of an Einstein? I really don't know. As you push back the frontiers of knowledge, what you need to know gets more and more extensive, the research gets harder and harder, the ideas more abstract, more difficult. In particular, the level of mathematics gets tougher and tougher. Einstein is often held up as a great mathematician but actually he wasn't terribly good at mathematics. He really wasn't a mathematician by training or temperament. To formulate his general theory of relativity he had to go to his friend Marcel Grossmann to teach him the necessary geometry to put it in an abstract form. What is happening now is that the trendy subjects I mentioned, like M-theory, string theory and so on, demand not only a lot of twentieth-century mathematics, but some twenty-first century mathematics too! In other words, the researchers are obliged to invent the mathematics as they go along. That makes it very difficult for one individual to make a decisive breakthrough.

## EINSTEIN'S LEGACY

**Phillip:**

Might they not need the assistance of one of those quantum mechanical computers we were talking about earlier?

**Paul:**

I don't think so. I believe that the fundamental laws of the universe are mathematically elegant and simple. Although they may be abstract, and although the branches of mathematics make it tough to learn and difficult for humans to grasp, nevertheless, at the end of the day, I think the ultimate laws will be elegantly simple. The point about computers is that they are very good at speedily solving messy, complicated problems. But computers are not very much help in this rarefied field of abstract mathematics.

## SELECTED READING

David Blair and Geoff McNamara, *Ripples on a Cosmic Sea*, Allen & Unwin, Sydney, 1997.

Paul Davies, *About Time*, Viking, London and Melbourne, 1995.

Paul Davies, *The Edge of Infinity* (revised edition), Penguin, Melbourne, 1994.

John Gribbin, *Timewarps*, Delacorte, New York, 1979.

John Gribbin and Michael White, *Einstein: A Life in Science*, Simon & Schuster, London, 1993.

Kip Thorne, *Black Holes and Time Warps*, Norton, New York, 1994.

Clifford Will, *Was Einstein Right?*, Basic Books, New York, 1986.

SIX

# Cosmic Butterflies

**Phillip:**

Ancient cultures viewed nature as a continual struggle between the forces of order and chaos. For two centuries scientists lay stress upon the order. Recently, however, chaos has been making a comeback. Nature can, it seems, be full of surprises. If ever there is a subject to bolster post-modern anxieties, to create the impression that everything is coming unstuck, it has to be the fashionable chaos theory. Yet, paradoxically, it seems that even chaos has an underlying structure, a hidden mathematical order.

**Paul:**

Newton had a famous image of the so-called clockwork universe. There is a well-known expression 'as regular as clockwork', which conveys the impression that the laws Newton discovered bestow upon nature some sort of mathematical dependability. I suppose the most obvious expression of that dependability is the orderly way in which the planets are supposed to move around the sun, but in principle it can be applied to every atom in every body in the universe.

COSMIC BUTTERFLIES

According to Newton's laws, there is a set of deterministic equations to describe all of nature, which means that everything is going to unfold 'according to plan', so to speak.

**Phillip:**

We've previously introduced Schrödinger's cat. It might be time to discuss another creature — Laplace's demon.

**Paul:**

Newton's clockwork universe image reached its pinnacle about a century later with the work of French mathematician and astronomer Pierre de Laplace. He realised that if Newton's laws should apply literally to every atom in the universe then, in a sense, the future of the universe must be fixed in advance. Laplace imagined some sort of cosmic super-intelligence, often known as Laplace's demon, which would be powerful enough not only to know where every atom was located and how it was moving, but could 'subject the data to analysis' — I think that was his expression. In other words, it could solve the equations and could figure out in advance where every atom was going to be in, say, a million years from now.

Now according to Newton's clockwork universe, and the underlying principles of Newtonian physics, it is possible, knowing the state of the universe exactly at one moment, to compute in detail its state at all subsequent moments — and,

## MORE BIG QUESTIONS

incidentally, at all previous moments. What this would mean, if it were true, is that everything that happens in the universe, including to human beings, right down to the wiggling of the tiniest finger, would already be fixed in advanced.

**Phillip:**
Reassuring but rather dull.

**Paul:**
Definitely dull. Ilya Prigogine, the Belgian chemist, summed it up rather poetically. He said such a scenario is rather like God being reduced to an archivist turning the pages of a cosmic history book that's already written.

**Phillip:**
In an earlier discussion you described the unpredictability of quantum mechanics. Is that the only limitation on predictability?

**Paul:**
The clockwork universe image might lead us to suppose that, if we had enough information about a system, it would be predictable in its infinite detail.

**Phillip:**
The stock market, roulette, what have you ...

## COSMIC BUTTERFLIES

**Paul:**

… Whatever it happens to be. Of course, we are surrounded by processes and systems that do seem to obey the laws of chance, rather than (or, more accurately, as well as) the laws of physics. Think, for example, of the pattern of raindrops on the ground, or the path of a lightning bolt. Casino managers make a healthy living depending on the laws of chance. The question is how can we fit these chancy, unpredictable things, like the movement of a roulette ball or the toss of a die, into the clockwork universe image. Are they compatible or is there some problem there? Well, people used to suppose that when you roll a die or something like that, if you could know in detail all the little forces that were operating, you could in principle predict the result. Should you toss a coin, then complete information about the system would enable you to determine in advance whether it was going to be heads or tails. However, what has been discovered this century is that there are circumstances in which a system can remain effectively unpredictable, however good our information gathering might be. We might know everything there is to know about the system, yet we still can't predict with certainty. Its behaviour is, in effect, random.

**Phillip:**

Enter the fashionable notion of chaos.

## MORE BIG QUESTIONS

**Paul:**

That's right. Chaos, or the theory of chaos, is certainly fashionable, but it is a concept that actually goes back about a century to the work of the French mathematical physicist Henri Poincaré. It was implicit in his mathematical study of Newtonian dynamics that there are some physical systems which are so exquisitely sensitive to minute disturbances that, effectively, they are unpredictable. Even though in principle these systems may obey a deterministic set of equations (that is, they are part of the clockwork universe), in practice you can never know their state at the level of detail necessary to predict what they are going to do.

**Phillip:**

Can you describe a practical example to demonstrate chaos?

**Paul:**

Imagine a ball attached to a piece of string. When I hold the free end of the string it makes a pendulum — we are back to the expression 'as regular as clockwork'. If I simply set it going, it has a certain natural frequency — tick, tock, tick, tock — very predictable. Now suppose I change the natural frequency a bit by wiggling the top of the string back and forth periodically in one direction — driving the pendulum, as we say *(see Fig. 6)*. If I drive the pendulum just above its natural frequency, it settles down into a stable pattern of

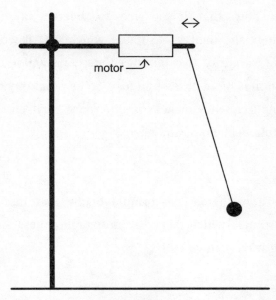

A ball is suspended from a string attached to a stand to form a pendulum free to swing in two dimensions. A motor drives the pendulum regularly back and forth in one direction at just above its natural swing frequency. The motion of the ball settles into a periodic clockwise or anticlockwise loop. If the driving frequency is slightly lowered, the motion of the ball becomes random, swinging a few times one way and then the other, with no predictable pattern.

motion. Although I am driving it in one direction, the ball swings in two dimensions, and traces out a sort of loop, an ellipse. It is very easy to predict, from one moment to the next, what is going to happen. But if I change the driving frequency a little and force the pendulum at slightly *below* its natural frequency, it goes haywire. Sometimes it swings to the right and sometimes it goes to the left. If you do the experiment properly in a laboratory, with a motor instead of my hand, the results are as I have just described. A careful analysis shows that, if you were to observe, say, four or five swings and then try to figure which way it would be swinging in one or two minutes time, you couldn't do it. The motion is more or less random. So just that tiny change in driving frequency makes the difference between regular, predictable behaviour, and chaos.

**Phillip:**

Is there a mathematical formula below that though? Is there a subtext which makes even its randomness, in some perverse way, predictable?

**Paul:**

By definition you can't reliably predict the future of random motion, but it is often said there is order in chaos. What this means is that there are certain similarities in different chaotic systems. We find chaos in many different types of physical systems. The pendulum is just one simple example. There are many others — dripping taps, variations in insect populations, fibrillating hearts, smoke trails — and a lot of them do seem to have a regular mathematical structure underpinning them, in the following sense. Although the actual motion itself may not be predictable, nevertheless the *onset* of chaos — when chaos will happen, and the way in which it is approached as you change, say, the driving frequency or the physical constraints — *that* can have mathematical regularity.

## COSMIC BUTTERFLIES

**Phillip:**

I'm thinking of Leonardo da Vinci trying to draw the flow of water over pebbles, or the visual experience of observing it. Utterly unpredictable and yet, after a while, there does seem to be a mathematical order to it.

**Paul:**

Turbulence is a very good example of order and chaos intermingled. Look at the swirling eddies in a turbulent stream and you see a classic example of chaos in action. If you try to predict where a little element of fluid is going to be at some later time, well, that's virtually impossible to do. There is another classic example with the great red spot of Jupiter. Jupiter is a giant gas planet, and as it rotates the gas swirls about and forms the distinctive coloured patterns one sees in photographs. Among these complex features created by fluid motion is the famous great red spot, a huge vortex the size of Earth. It is a coherent structure but, again, if you take any given element of gas and try to follow it through that red spot, the motion of the gas becomes unpredictable. So there is a sort of amalgam of order and chaos in these examples. Today it is very fashionable to apply chaos theory to turbulence in the hope of understanding it better.

People used to suppose that complicated behaviour demanded complicated causes. What chaos theory shows is

MORE BIG QUESTIONS

that you can get very complicated behaviour from very simple causes. The little pendulum movement that I described illustrates this very well.

**Phillip:**

Paul, I seem to hear the approach of a butterfly.

**Paul:**

There is something called the butterfly effect, which has become rather famous of late. I mentioned that a chaotic system behaves randomly because it is so exquisitely sensitised to minute disturbances that we effectively cannot predict what is going to happen. All the little twists and turns of fate would have to be followed if we were to know what is going to happen next. This effect was first discovered, as I mentioned, by Henri Poincaré, but it was first made explicit many years later by Edward Lorenz in the United States, when the first electronic computers were used to model air flow as part of the attempt to forecast the weather. Of course weather forecasting is notoriously bad; the weather is notoriously unpredictable. We now realise that there is a very good reason for this. When I was a student everybody supposed that if you could just have a big enough computer and gather enough data you would be able to work out accurate long-range weather forecasts. But this simply isn't so for a chaotic system. If the weather is so incredibly

## COSMIC BUTTERFLIES

sensitised to tiny disturbances, then the mere flap of a butterfly's wings in, say, Adelaide today could affect the course of a hurricane in the United States next week. Hence 'the butterfly effect', as it has been dubbed.

**Phillip:**
But it is a metaphor, not a fact.

**Paul:**
Oh, it is a fact. The whole point about a chaotic system is that it really does depend on such minute disturbances; that's what makes it unpredictable. It is *not*, however, a matter of saying 'Well all we need to do is study a particular butterfly and we will be able to forecast the motion of that hurricane'. The butterfly effect implies that the motion of the hurricane depends on squillions of such tiny disturbances. The unpredictability arises because we cannot possibly know *every* minute influence.

**Phillip:**
It seems to me to have infinite applicability to human affairs, to international affairs, because often in history we have seen a couple of major powers trying desperately to avoid war, only to have some tiny little incident, totally misinterpreted, trigger devastation.

## MORE BIG QUESTIONS

**Paul:**

There have been many examples where human society is driven to the edge of chaos, so that the slightest trigger can direct one course of action or another, maybe totally changing the course of human history. I guess you only have to think of Sarajevo, and the assassination of the Archduke Ferdinand that triggered World War I. The question is, can we write down a set of equations that will somehow, if not predict the outcome of historical instabilities, at least determine when such instabilities are likely to arise?

**Phillip:**

A lot of prime ministers would be grateful if you could.

**Paul:**

This is really important. I think we have to accept that if a system becomes chaotic, there is nothing we can do to predict the outcome, but we may at least be able to predict when chaos is going to occur. It might perhaps be possible to determine that this or that state of affairs is becoming very dangerous because such-and-such a parameter is being pushed to the point where it is going to hit the chaotic regime. We can readily imagine this in economics. We can imagine looking at the complicated output of the stock market, the gold price, currency fluctuations and so on and, if we are clever enough, being able to conclude: 'If we go far enough

COSMIC BUTTERFLIES

down this path, if the gold price falls too far, say, we are going to hit a chaotic regime, and then we won't know what's going to happen next'. Many former scientists are now employed on Wall Street and in the City of London applying chaos theory and related mathematics to financial markets.

I like to say that the global economy is an example of a self-organising system. A lot of people fondly imagine that politicians and economists set the levers of the economic machine and drive it; that they know what is going on; that the economy is like a predictable mechanistic system. So if they only get the lever settings right they will drive it and steer it in a certain predictable direction to a desirable goal. But I think that is a load of nonsense. I think that the world economy (since it has now become globalised) is really a self-organising system. It has taken on a life of its own. It has its own dynamic, its own freedom, and all that is happening when economists and politicians 'set the levers' is that they are reacting to events. They don't actually have a great deal of choice in the matter.

**Phillip:**

Yes, but they don't actually admit to this, and of course they are sorely afflicted by hubris. This may be one of the virtues of chaos theory in that it makes all of us a little more modest. If there is one profession that learns to live with chaos theory I think it would have to be politics. That

## MORE BIG QUESTIONS

makes me wonder whether, out of the prognostications about chaos, some useful tools will emerge?

**Paul:**

There is a lot of interest in applying chaos theory to sociology, politics or, in particular, economics. This raises the tantalising question of whether you can make money by applying chaos theory to the stock market? Consider these little wiggles and jiggles in the record of the stock price or the gold price or whatever. Is there a mathematical formula that can show us what is going on? To a certain extent it is clear that markets are chaotic systems, or that they have periods where they go chaotic, but there are also periods where they appear to be more orderly and predictable.

**Phillip:**

Or when the pendulum swings. It is a common expression to describe the behaviour of the markets.

**Paul:**

Yes. So I think we might have an 'edge of chaos' phenomenon here. Some people do indeed claim that by applying the mathematics of chaos theory to the financial markets they understand them better, and even make money from doing it. This is big business now.

**Phillip:**

Let's be oxymoronic and talk about *organised* chaos, if there is such a thing.

**Paul:**

The relationship between chaos and organisation, or self-organisation, is rather deep. Let me give you another example which is a favourite of mine. Take a saucepan of water, put it on the stove and heat it from beneath. The fluid in the saucepan is at first totally featureless, but after a while, as the temperature difference between the bottom and the top of the pan builds up, the fluid starts to convect. If you do this carefully and look on it from above, you see an orderly pattern of hexagonal convection cells. The water spontaneously forms this hexagonal pattern. We call that self-organisation. If you go on heating, and the temperature difference becomes greater, the fluid starts to boil and it becomes chaotic. The same type of physical system, the same type of mathematics, that leads to self-organisation on the one hand also leads to chaos. These phenomena are widespread — from lasers to chemical mixtures to ant colonies. The same mathematical principles seem to apply.

**Phillip:**

You mentioned the edge of chaos. Can we dwell on that edge for a moment?

## MORE BIG QUESTIONS

**Paul:**

The example that I gave with the pendulum illustrates the edge of chaos quite well. If the pendulum is driven at one frequency its motion is orderly; if it is driven at another it becomes chaotic, so as you change the driving frequency you approach the edge of chaos. In many examples of chaotic systems you find that, as you approach the chaotic regime, the behaviour progressively shifts from regular to less and less predictable. There is a virtue in this sin, in that chaos can also have a creative aspect. What is chaos, after all? Unpredictability. But chaos also, in a sense, creates an openness, a freedom, to the future. On the edge of chaos one can get the best of both worlds. One has the constraint of the orderly regime, but the openness of the chaotic regime. Some people, like Stuart Kauffman, the American biophysicist, have suggested that nature's creativity in the biological domain perhaps exploits this edge of chaos phenomenon. Evolution serves to move species and ecosystems to the edge, where they are then poised between order and chaos, thus having the openness of being able to explore new pathways, which may not have been predicted, and yet not descending into total anarchy.

**Phillip:**

Is there any evidence that evolution is working to a plan? Or are the splendid variety of life forms essentially random?

# COSMIC BUTTERFLIES

**Paul:**

This is a really fundamental question. When Darwin published his theory of evolution he upset the Church, as is well known. A lot of religious people were deeply offended by the notion that human beings have descended from more primitive life forms; they worried particularly about being descended from apes. But some sought comfort in Darwin's own theory by putting forward the notion of a ladder of progress, the idea that evolution began with microbes and ended with Man. They perceived in the evolutionary process an upward trend, claiming that over the billions of years that evolution has worked its magic there has been a process of 'advancement'. They were able to interpret this as evidence that evolution was *directed* towards the emergence of something like human beings. That gave people some comfort — to think that they were the end product of a long, complicated process, but a process nevertheless with a goal, the goal being humanity. So they could still retain some vestige of the privileged status that they thought humans had before Darwin came along and upset the apple cart.

These days biologists hate this sort of terminology; they hate the notion of a ladder of progress. You often see this depiction of a shambling ape gradually becoming more upright until it evolves into *Homo erectus* or *Homo sapiens*. Such cartoons convey the impression, forcefully

## More Big Questions

denied by biologists, that there was a trend towards, in expectation of, the emergence of human beings. But there is really no hard evidence at all of any directionality in evolution. It is the essence of Darwin's theory that nature has no foresight — it cannot look ahead and anticipate what might be needed. Nature is blind, changes occur at random, and the changes that confer some advantage at any particular time get selected. But there is no end goal, no directionality, to this whole process. At least that is the biologists' current position.

**Phillip:**
In a word, are we chemical freaks or are we the consequence of a bio-friendly cosmos?

**Paul:**
My own inclination is that we live in a bio-friendly cosmos, that life emerges naturally as part of the outworking of the basic laws of the universe, and that life will occur often under the right circumstances. But this is pure conjecture.

**Phillip:**
This question is a leap in the dark but is there any relevance between chaos theory and artificial intelligence?

## COSMIC BUTTERFLIES

**Paul:**

I long ago came to the conclusion that our sense of freedom, our sense of free will, comes from an edge of chaos phenomenon. Free will basically means we can't predict our own behaviour. We feel that there is an openness, that we have alternatives. Yet again there is not total anarchy. I don't suddenly feel that I have no idea whether I am going to leap out of this chair and dance a jig.

And yet I don't precisely know what I am going to say next. So this sense of openness, of freedom, does seem to be something to do with an edge of chaos phenomenon. When you look at the operation of the brain it has various instabilities, it is operating on the edge of a number of instabilities that could be associated with the sense of freedom that we all have. As a vastly complex neural net, the brain is highly sensitised to input data from eyes, ears and other sensory collectors, yet it is not completely unstable. So I think the edge of chaos concept does apply to the human brain, and probably to artificial intelligence too, if we're to give it the sort of creativity that human beings actually have.

**Phillip:**

It sometimes seems that scientific theories are like fads. They suddenly explode, there is a great deal of discussion on them, and they ebb away. Is chaos theory in fact exhausting itself?

## More Big Questions

### Paul:

In the early days I think people saw chaos everywhere. Once it was discovered that a chaotic system could be as simple as a driven pendulum, they looked around and they saw chaos in everything in sight. The American physicist Joseph Ford wrote that non-chaotic systems were as scarce as hens' teeth. I think that is a bit of an exaggeration. Quite clearly there are systems that are orderly and predictable; the solar system mostly falls into that category. But we do see chaos out there, for example, in the asteroid belts. Some asteroids move along orbits that are basically chaotic, and eventually get flung out of the solar system altogether. I think we have to acknowledge that we live in a world that is a complex mixture of order and chaos. There are those phenomena that are predictable, and those that are unpredictable, and they can be tangled together in a very intimate way. It is not just a matter of saying, 'Well this lot of phenomena over here is going to be orderly and predictable, and display clockwork-type behaviour, while all the rest is going to be chaotic'. Very often the same type of physical system can become chaotic under only slightly different circumstances from when it is orderly.

### Phillip:

Human creativity and free will. When you feel your own mental processes, such as they are, you have a feeling that

## COSMIC BUTTERFLIES

chaos theory is applicable right there. Einstein talked about intuitively struggling with a massive notion but being unable to find it. He went to sleep, woke up in the morning, and there it was! Can this be a part of the chaos within our neurones and synapses?

**Paul:**

Oh yes, I think that there is a subconscious level where we can work things out without being aware of doing so. I am a great devotee of crossword puzzles, and I will often get stuck on a clue, fall asleep, and the next morning instantly the answer is there. It's as if some part of my brain has been working on the problem without my knowing about it. Often, if I am stumped with a problem, maybe a mathematical problem, I will just go and do something else for a bit — fiddle around in the garden or something of that sort. I find it very helpful to get my mind off the immediate problem, and then when I go back to it again it is much easier, the answer seems to have appeared spontaneously.

**Phillip:**

The process of imagination is a constant one of stirring up a bit of chaos in your own mind, isn't it, and then hoping something will come out of it?

## MORE BIG QUESTIONS

**Paul:**

Yes, indeed. I remember Fred Hoyle once remarking that if he was stuck on a scientific problem, he would go walking in the hills, would allow his thoughts to be scattered. Then when they fell back together again, they might make a different arrangement, and the problem would be solved. I think you are quite right; stirring the pot, or stirring the ideas, sums it up well. After all, creativity is all about doing something new. The essence of chaos theory is that we don't know what is going to come next. The future is unpredictable, we are going into something new, which wasn't foretold. If we desire human creativity, or creativity in nature, there has got to be an element of unpredictability — but it mustn't be total anarchy. There has to be some sort of amalgam of order and chaos, like the edge of chaos phenomenon that we've talked about.

All this discussion of human creativity raises what I think is the biggest of the big questions, which is this: how can human beings make any sense at all of the world that they live in? Why does the universe have enough order for us to discern an underlying lawfulness, and yet enough chaos to permit such things as nature's openness and human free will? The chaos theorist Joseph Ford once remarked to me that he liked to think of God as a sort of river-boat gambler, the kind of guy you could sit down and have a drink with! What he meant by this was that the

## COSMIC BUTTERFLIES

unpredictable element in nature can be a source of joy. And I think he is quite right that 'life, the universe and everything' does have a chaotic element. But I also believe that there is a deeper principle at work as well, a principle which somehow harnesses the openness of chaos, and provides a felicitous amalgam of order and chaos, an amalgam that in some sense represents the best of all possible worlds.

## SELECTED READING

Peter Convey and Roger Highfield, *Frontiers and Complexity*, Faber & Faber, London, 1995.

Jack Cohen and Ian Stewart, *The Collapse of Chaos*, Viking, London, 1994.

Paul Davies, *The Cosmic Blueprint*, Heinemann, London, 1988.

James Gleick, *Chaos*, Simon & Schuster, New York, 1987.

Ilya Prigogine and Isabelle Stengers, *Order Out of Chaos*, Heinemann, London, 1984.

Ian Stewart, *Does God Play Dice?*, Blackwell, Oxford, 1989.